I0823005

Healing the Oppressed Body

Healing the Oppressed Body

A THERAPEUTIC GUIDE FOR RADICAL SELF-LIBERATION

Andrea Gutiérrez-Glik, LCSW

PENGUIN LIFE

VIKING
An imprint of Penguin Random House LLC
1745 Broadway, New York, NY 10019
penguinrandomhouse.com

A Penguin Life Book

VIKING and VIKING ship colophon are registered trademarks of Penguin Random House LLC.

Book design by Daniel Lagin

LIBRARY OF CONGRESS CONTROL NUMBER: 2025028228

ISBN 9780593656761 (hardcover)
ISBN 9780593656778 (ebook)

Printed in the United States of America
1st Printing

The authorized representative in the EU for product safety and compliance is Penguin Random House Ireland, Morrison Chambers, 32 Nassau Street, Dublin D02 YH68, Ireland, https://eu-contact.penguin.ie.

To my clients and my consultees.

Thank you for your trust, your raw vulnerability.

None of this exists or means anything without you.

A note about case examples: The case examples in this book are an amalgamation of fifteen years of client work. No case example reflects one client in particular, and any identifying info has been significantly altered. If you are a past or current client and see yourself in one of these characters, please know that I have seen hundreds of clients with similar issues and identities. I have done the best of my ability to honor you and everyone else I have worked with within these pages. I cherish and respect you all beyond words.

CONTENTS

PART 3

UNDERSTANDING AND HEALING FROM *YOUR* TRAUMA

PART 4

NOW WHAT?

Introduction

When I was twenty-one years old, I started seeing a therapist. I had just fully come out, leaving the last relationship that had tethered me to the confines and semi-comfort of heterosexuality. While I had slept with women before, this breakup with a boyfriend allowed me to finally give myself over to the queer unknown and all it held.

It was a rough time. My straight friend group saw me as the "bad guy" for breaking up with my boyfriend. My family said they were grieving what they thought my life was going to be—following in their footsteps with a normative relationship and life trajectory. I felt certain about who I was but trapped and scared at the same time. Jumping headfirst into queer dating was terrifying. Would I ever be as loved or as safe as I thought I had been with a cisgender man? Would I ever find stability with a queer or trans person? What would life as a gay woman even look like?

I needed support; I needed to process that breakup and all that was unfolding in my life. But working at a sex toy store while finishing up college meant I was pretty much broke. So I found a therapist who took my insurance and had availability. Those were my only criteria.

The therapist was an older straight white woman who specialized in trauma. She soon became convinced that my father had sexually abused me and that was why I was a lesbian. She told me, "I think I know where your fear of penises comes from." This wasn't based on anything I had said or even alluded to. I wasn't afraid of penises; in fact, I worked in a store that proudly displayed an entire table of them in every shape and size! I had never felt so misunderstood in my life. It was hard enough to be fully coming out and coming into my queerness, experiencing the trauma of my family's and society's homophobia, and reckoning with the impact of six years of dating and having sex with men as a closeted gay woman. To have my sexuality be so misconstrued, reduced to something that wasn't even accurate, was devastating. What's more, for years to come, I was plagued with intrusive images of abuse that had never actually occurred.

It's no surprise that I stopped seeing that therapist and avoided therapy for years. I have since realized that coming out as a lesbian was only a piece of the whole that I was struggling to understand. I had inherited trauma as the granddaughter of persecuted people, I had terrible OCD and anxiety, I was addicted to alcohol, and I was profoundly impacted by the death of my cousin in a car crash when we were young. Not to mention growing up in a society that shamed women's sexuality, queerness, and any body that wasn't thin. I had starved myself physically, emotionally, and sexually for years. But none of those issues was addressed in the therapy room because I had been unseen and shamed.

After my negative experience, I stopped believing in the potential of therapy. Instead, it was the queer and trans folks around me who guided me through the process of being fully out. My lovers and friends were the ones who gave me what I needed: space to question what a queer life would mean for me, space to cry and scream about the blatant homophobia I experienced, space to feel and be validated.

With them, I learned to love my queerness, to finally accept my abundant body and neurodivergent brain. Understanding how essential community had been to my healing, I went to school to get a master's in social work, preparing for a career as a community organizer.

At the time, it didn't occur to me to seek out a therapist who was also queer; I wasn't even aware that was an option. It wasn't until grad school that I finally met with a queer therapist after losing a dear friend to suicide. The friend had been a lover and a queer mentor to me. I was so deep in grief that I felt I had no other choice but to seek therapy.

That first therapeutic relationship with a queer therapist changed my life. It showed me therapy could be a safe place for me as a queer woman and for everyone who has felt marginalized. This experience helped me understand even more the importance of being fully understood and seen in therapy. It even eventually drew me to the one-on-one work I do with clients now.

Everyone, especially those with oppressed bodies—whether we are marginalized for our identities or our differences—needs to be seen and accepted for who we are, to be embraced physically and emotionally, and to be given the safe space to heal. Queer community saved me, and helped me find my true sense of self as a lesbian woman. And not just because I figured out my sexuality but because the things about me that had never quite fit anywhere—my queerness, my body and brain, my difference—were loved, seen, and held. And it was that first queer therapist who helped me see the need for more representation in the mental health community.

The right therapist and the right community can provide you space to be held and to heal. They are downright lifesaving for oppressed and marginalized communities who have experienced the trauma of feeling unseen and unsafe—people of color, immigrants, women, neurodivergent folks, anti-capitalists, anyone horrified by war and violence and the blatant destruction of Earth by their fellow humans. For those who have experienced homophobia, transphobia, racism, sexism, religious discrimination, ableism, generational trauma, and more, it is vital to understand why we hurt and how we can heal.

WHY WE MIGHT NOT TRUST THERAPY

The world of therapy has long failed to look at the unique trauma caused by oppression. In fact, therapy has a tragic history of *itself* being a source of trauma for those of us at the margins.

LGBTQ+ people were criminalized and/or institutionalized in psych wards for hundreds of years across the US, and they continue to be in many parts of the world. Today in the US, trans people continue to be criminalized, denied health care, and, for trans youth, at risk of being taken from their homes. The predominant "treatment" for queer and trans folks used to be electroconvulsive therapy (ECT)—which at the time was a severe procedure with extreme cognitive implications. (Today's ECT is milder and is only used with the client's informed consent when they are resistant to other treatments, often for severe depression, suicidality, and psychosis.) Conversion therapy, a traumatizing and non-evidence-based "treatment" that attempts to "cure" people of their queerness and transness, is still used today, and is still legal in about half of the US. And I'm not just talking about religious conversion therapy or camps—it is still used by some psychotherapists and psychiatrists as well.

Many of my clients who are processing religious trauma have had traumatizing experiences with therapists who do not disclose that their therapy style is deeply influenced by homophobic and transphobic Christian "values." To be clear, Christianity is not the only religion that perpetuates harmful beliefs about queer and trans people. Many of the world's organized religions are homophobic or became that way due to the impact of colonialism and extremism, and there are plenty of secular cultures saturated with homophobic biases.

Today, trans folks also face additional challenges. While cisgender people are able to make whatever changes they please to their bodies without being evaluated by a mental health professional, trans people often must go through exploitative, humiliating, and expensive psychotherapy to access hormone therapy and gender-affirming care, and have faced hundreds of bills attacking their health care.

Queer and trans folks aren't the only ones for whom psychotherapy feels unsafe and inaccessible. The centuries-long history of medical experimentation on people of color has left whole communities wary of psychotherapy. People living with chronic illnesses also have reasons to not trust psychotherapy. Many of my clients have been told that their chronic illness and pain are all in their heads. Those of us with abundant bodies have long found therapy to be a site of body violence and shame. Those who are disabled and neurodiverse have also avoided therapy due to the near impossibility of finding therapists who share their experience.

Therapy hasn't been accessible to poor and working-class folks either. Many are only able to access mental health care through nonprofits, if at all, as most private practices, mine included, either don't take insurance or are priced in a way that is impossible for anyone without disposable income. Nonprofits can certainly provide good mental health care; however, these counseling centers often have long waiting lists and offer little choice in which therapist clients work with, which is especially important for anyone who wants and needs their identities to be reflected in their therapist. I have clients who sought in-network or free counseling, only to discover the organization itself had religious and homophobic values that were not disclosed.

So of course those of us at the margins feel therapy isn't for us. Why would we spend our time, money, and emotional energy on something that doesn't see our identities clearly, that doesn't even consider our trauma to be real?

WHAT IS OPPRESSION-BASED TRAUMA?

Oppression, the systematic domination of one group by another, is dehumanizing. It results in a lack of basic human rights, and even access to essential resources like food and housing and safety. To be oppressed is to be forced into experiencing a diminished sense of self and worthiness. We feel like it is not safe to be ourselves, and so we fracture our inner selves in order to survive. The shock waves of trauma that we feel are as real as those of any experience that has long been recognized as trauma.

Historically, oppression hasn't been considered to be trauma. But that's finally changing. It is high time to name the truth: Oppression-based trauma is real and devastating.

There are many books on trauma healing that have changed my life and my clients' lives. Yet, when my clients have asked for recommendations for books that reflected their own experiences as a queer or trans person—books that name the daily oppression we experience as trauma—there was not a single book I could suggest. There was little or nothing that spoke to the specific traumas those in my community experience: homophobia, transphobia, "corrective" sexual abuse, institutional injustices, medical trauma, body dysphoria, being deadnamed and misgendered, or growing up in a religion that sees you as an abomination.

In a recent Gallup poll, 10 percent of millennials and 20 percent of Gen Z identified as LGBTQ+: How is it that we make up such a significant percentage of the population of these core generations, and yet there is nothing out there written specifically for us and our healing journeys?

We're not alone. People with disabilities and chronic illnesses face isolation and discrimination at every turn. People living in poverty—of any race, gender, ability, or sexuality—live through the daily trauma of not having their basic needs met, or in fear of losing them at any time. The world of therapy has only just begun to crack the surface of the ongoing traumas people of color survive every day living in a white supremacist world, and the ways centuries of violence have manifested in people's bodies and our society as a whole.

The Trauma Symptoms of Discrimination Scale (TSDS)[1] is a recently developed psychological tool used to measure symptoms of oppression-based trauma such as nervous system dysregulation, feeling disconnected and isolated from others, and negative changes in cognition and mood. Not surprisingly, these are the same symptoms listed in the PTSD Checklist for *DSM-5** (PCL-5), a tool for assessing PTSD and its severity. In a study[2] using the TSDS, 97 percent of the participants who were people of color reported racial discrimination that led to traumatic stress. Additionally, 86 percent of participants experienced discrimination that led to traumatic stress based on disability, 81 percent based on their sexuality, 68 percent based on their religion, 56 percent based on their age, 38 percent based on their social class, and 31 percent based on their gender. All oppressed people live with the impact of discrimination, in their physical and emotional bodies.

As we'll learn in the coming pages, stress from discrimination shows up in the body as trauma and triggers the same protective and adaptive responses the body uses to keep us safe after any trauma. Add to this the fact that people often experience multiple oppressions due to their intersecting identities, and you can see how these add up—the more oppression one experiences, the more trauma and more

*The *DSM* is the American Psychiatric Association's *Diagnostic and Statistical Manual.*

stress on the body. For example, my clients who are queer and trans people of color face the ongoing stress of white supremacy and homophobia or transphobia on a daily basis. It's nearly impossible for them to experience safety and stability in the here and now.

With all of the research on the chronic stress of oppression, we know what it does to someone's mental and physical health. Yet many therapists do not and are not yet trained to acknowledge these experiences as trauma, making therapy for many marginalized clients uncomfortable at best, and catastrophic at worst.

WE NEED TO VIEW TRAUMA HEALING THROUGH AN ANTI-OPPRESSIVE LENS

In these dire days, it is frankly not enough to see trauma healing as a depoliticized act. When we heal from oppression and trauma, it is an inherently political act. It is an act of resistance to the systems that have abused us, that want to see us as broken and complacent. Take, for example, the fact that a symptom of a patriarchal society is rape and sexual abuse. Every time one of my clients heals from sexual violence, they are participating in an act of resistance to that patriarchal system. They are able to be in the world in a new way, one that has a ripple effect on everyone around them. Now, what if trauma healing was framed in this same way? Not just as psychotherapy, not just as a popular topic on social media, but as political resistance? What if we saw "individual healing" as a form of collective healing because of what it allows us to go out into the world and do? What if we viewed our own healing through an anti-oppressive lens? Our healing becomes rebellion against oppression. And it makes our communities stronger, meaning as *we* heal individually, we *all* heal collectively on a larger scale.

With *Healing the Oppressed Body*, I'm proposing a reenvisioning of how we look at healing. I look at oppression-based trauma, intergenerational trauma, and the trauma of "modern living" as traumatic experiences we are all dealing with. Instead of considering only culturally acknowledged traumas—like sexual assaults and abuse, accidents and disasters, and active combat—my approach instead acknowledges them as one type of trauma among many.

We cannot fully heal from trauma without acknowledging the role that oppression plays. We must see how those of us at the margins are more likely to experience trauma both interpersonally and systematically. We must understand how it lives in our bodies and is carried through generations. We must acknowledge how we contain within us not only our life experiences but also our ancestors'.

To heal from the real trauma that is caused by oppression, we must call it what it is. We deserve to see ourselves reflected in the trauma field and to have healing tools that are attuned to our particular life experiences. That's why I wrote this book. While I specialize in working with my own community of queer and trans folks, anyone at the margins who experiences the trauma of structural oppression is welcome in these pages, as our struggles and our healing are intricately bound up in each other's.

THE THREE CORE BRANCHES OF TRAUMA HEALING FOR RADICAL SELF-LIBERATION

Both inside of therapy and outside in our daily lives, we heal through what is uniquely impactful for LGBTQ+ folks and all of us at the margins—what I call the three core branches of trauma healing: compassion, freedom, and community.

Compassion for ourselves and others, compassion for all past versions of ourselves, compassion for our bodies and nervous systems, compassion for our childhood selves and our ancestors. Compassion for our hardworking nervous systems that keep us safe. Compassion for those in our community who are acting from a place of survival and harm as we are all dealing with our own trauma and want to heal.

Freedom in our bodies—such as through sex, BDSM, body mod, dance, performance, creativity, activism, or being in nature. Freedom from the burdens we carry. Freedom to love and be loved. Freedom in all parts of our psyche. Self-liberation to find and love our true self.

Community with all aspects of ourselves—our past and younger selves, as well as outer community with peer groups, microcommunities, and the natural world around us. Community with people who match your freak, your spiritual and political leanings. Community with people nothing like you who happen to be your neighbor or who you meet at the movies. Community with chosen family, online communities, and people who have the capacity and ability to love and accept you.

These three core branches of healing are at the heart of each of the therapeutic modalities and methods I present in the pages to come.

WHAT YOU'LL FIND ON OUR JOURNEY

In the following pages, I'll share what I have witnessed to be most transformative for my clients and community. This includes both traditional and cutting-edge evidence-based techniques from the world of trauma therapy as well as alternative avenues. You'll also discover that many of my approaches are somatic, meaning "of the body." Part of being a trauma therapist for marginalized folks is working with and acknowledging the body, not just the mind. I believe that our bodies are where we get free, both inside the therapeutic space and outside of it.

Our bodies respond to trauma instinctively, and yes, our bodies keep the score of our past and ongoing trauma. However, we are miraculously resilient creatures and we are not doomed to suffer from our trauma forever. In part 1, Understanding the Basics of Trauma's Impacts, I'll share the science of how our brains and nervous systems process trauma, showing how the nervous system is designed to keep us safe at all costs and can trick us into feeling like we are reexperiencing trauma. You'll learn techniques and exercises to calm your stressed-out nervous system so that the very physical chemical responses to triggers don't overwhelm you. You'll read about how your brain stores traumatic memories and how you can actually rewrite your own story through something called neuroplasticity. You'll see how our go-to coping behaviors may actually be getting in the way of healing and how, with repetition and new experiences, you can create what's called a mismatch—a way to retrain your brain that I promise will change your life.

In part 2, Two Foundational Theories Behind Trauma Healing for Our Oppressed Bodies, we'll explore *attachment theory* and *parts theory.* Attachment theory is the river at the bottom of the ocean of *any* therapeutic work. Our attachment experiences completely shape our sense of self—in particular our feelings of worthiness and belonging, which are especially key when it comes to existing at the margins. And we can't work with trauma fully without acknowledging how it fragments us from parts of ourselves, leading to structural dissociation. In this context, *dissociation* is more than just "checking out" or not being inside our bodies. It actually means to be cut off from entire parts of ourselves. Healing means rejoining with these parts.

You'll also learn how to recognize your inner parts—including your child self, or even selves, who may be too frightened to make themselves known to you. Everyone has inner parts, but folks on the margins have had to fragment ourselves even more so in order to survive. Some parts of us feel literally unsafe to show themselves. In these pages, we'll walk through how to invite all your internal parts to come forward, unburden themselves, and feel safe.

In part 3, Understanding and Healing from *Your* Trauma, with the theory of parts 1 and 2 under your belt, you'll begin to walk down your own path to trauma healing. I'll share modalities for beginning to heal from daily oppression, childhood trauma, the trauma of "modern living," and the ancestral trauma you may carry in your genes. And always, throughout the book, I will give you strategies and exercises that you can do on your own and with a therapist. Finally, we'll end by sharing resources and guidance for your next steps.

As I guide you through the different theories and modalities to facilitate your own healing journey, I'll introduce client examples along the way. These examples are amalgamations of the beautiful, resilient, and expansive people I have had the honor of working with as a therapist—all of whom have experienced trauma, and all of whom hold identities that have long been left out of the conversation around trauma healing.

WHY WE NEED TRAUMA HEALING FOR OUR OPPRESSED BODIES *NOW*

These are desperate and frightening times, especially for those of us at the margins. Trauma healing has to be as radical and as urgent as any movement in the streets. We need to understand the impact of stress and trauma on our nervous system *now*, we need to feel more whole and compassionate toward ourselves *now*, we need to feel freedom in our lives and bodies *now*, we need to feel in community with others *now*.

While things have greatly improved for queer and trans folks since the 1950s, I have clients who get denied basic medical care every day. Prescriptions for hormones get mysteriously deleted at their pharmacy, letters of referral for gender-affirming surgery to be covered are denied, contractors refuse to work on someone's home because they are an openly gay couple. Yes, people can be more out and proud, but it literally comes at a cost. My clients who are people of color physically do not feel safe under white supremacy. The toll that takes on their bodies and sense of self is profound. My sick and disabled clients get labeled crazy, defiant, and lazy, and because of it, aren't getting the lifesaving care they need.

"It's not just this," my clients tell me. They remind me the world is also literally on fire. People are still denying the long-term impact of COVID. People are genocided. The climate continues to collapse. Masses suffer. The richest 1 percent own more wealth than 95 percent of humanity.

All of this can make people feel hopeless, powerless, extremely depressed, and anxious.

So where do we find the hope?

When we do the work to heal ourselves, when we practice trauma healing for our oppressed bodies, we can walk back out into the world with a greater capacity to support ourselves and others.

This is where I see the hope. In this overwhelming, out-of-control world, what we *can* control is how we care for ourselves and how that in turn allows us to care for others.

I'm excited that you are joining me on the journey. Let's get started.

YOUR TURN

Checking In with Your Body

Psychology has long separated the mind and the body from each other. But in my view, it is essential that our bodies come along for the ride. Since trauma manifests in our bodies, they are also the site of where we heal. Throughout this book, I'll invite you to check in with your body. This is something you might have experience with, or you may feel new to this invitation. Below is our first exercise.

Bring to mind a positive memory. This could be a life highlight or a nice everyday experience that feels really warm and safe. In this memory, what do you see, hear, smell, feel, maybe even taste? Bring yourself into this experience with all your senses and take a few deep breaths.

Once you are there in the positive memory, take a second and check in with your jaw. Maybe you even bring your fingertips there. When you press down on your jaw with your fingers, does your jaw muscle feel hard and tight, or soft and loose? Notice that.

Refocus your awareness on your memory. Now check in with your throat. Is it easy or hard to swallow? Next, take a breath. Is it effortless to take a deep breath in, or do you find yourself shallow breathing only into your throat?

Refocus your awareness on your memory. Now place a hand on your heart. Bring awareness to your heart space. Does it feel open like energy could pour in or out or does it feel closed, like there is a wall in front of your heart? Does it hurt or is it warm?

Come back to that memory again. Move your hand to your

gut. Does it feel sick or calm? Rooted or queasy? Notice any other sensations.

Thinking of the memory once more, bring your awareness to your hands and feet. Do they want to move? Do they feel heavy or light? Do they feel buzzy or calm? Are they sweaty or dry?

And finally, scan your body for any other missed sensations while you think of your memory.

This is one way to get in touch with your body's sensations. The more you notice your body and the internal signals you receive from it, the easier it will be to stay connected to, take care of, and enjoy your somatic self. This attunement to your body's messages takes time, especially in a world that encourages us to disconnect from our physical experience all day, every day. With time, the more you notice your body, the more ingrained those networks in your brain will become to tune in versus tune out your body. Be gentle and compassionate with yourself when it's hard to listen to your body, and remember you have basically been trained to ignore it. Tuning in is a radical act of resistance.

With each exercise I introduce, you can check in with your body—or anytime you want to sit, think about something you've just read, take a pause. Because remember, we want your body to come along for the ride.

PART 1

UNDERSTANDING THE BASICS OF TRAUMA'S IMPACTS

CHAPTER 1

How Our Bodies Respond to Trauma

What brings you to therapy right now? This is a standard question that most therapists ask their prospective new clients.

Many of my clients come to me wanting to feel better and recognizing that past trauma is getting in the way. Some clients only want to focus on the here and now and what's unfolding for them presently. Yet that work never feels as effective or deep. For each of us, there is always more beneath the surface. The trauma we've endured grows roots deep into other aspects of our current lives.

When I use the word *trauma*, what exactly do I mean? Trauma is any experience that makes us feel we are in danger—one that leaves a lasting impact on us, shaping our beliefs about ourselves, the world, and our ability to feel safe. Traumatic experiences can vary from a single incident, meaning an event that occurred once, like a sexual assault or a car accident, to ongoing traumas like chronic or prolonged illness, unsafe or abusive childhoods, growing up in a war zone, or living in a society that doesn't view you or treat you as human.

Jessy came to see me because she was feeling unable to manage her anxiety. As a trans woman, Jessy felt like she was preparing for battle every time she left her apartment, even with her white privilege. Her heart rate increased, her palms got sweaty: the classic fight-or-flight response. When she was on the subway every morning, each time a commuter stared at her or made a transphobic comment, she felt her body surge with hot energy, as if someone had threatened her life. When people refuse to see us as human, it provokes a survival response. When people or systems don't see our humanity, we are more at risk for both state and interpersonal violence. Jessy's nervous system picked up on that every second of every day, and it, of course, had long-term effects on her body.

In this chapter, I'm going to introduce you to your wildly adaptive nervous system. Understanding how and why your body makes you *feel* the way you do is essential to understanding your trauma. Along with Jessy, you'll learn techniques to feel calm and aware. This is called the *stabilization* phase of therapy because it is when your body learns to experience just enough safety that it can take the next step in healing—trauma *processing*. During processing, clients dive directly into their trauma, hopefully in a guided and structured way to help them understand how it impacts them, and then how to make new meaning from those experiences. After processing, belief systems shift, and the body calms down and experiences fewer triggers and flashbacks. This is the *integration* phase where healing occurs. Trauma processing is intense work, and you can't process your trauma if you're not stabilized because doing so will destabilize you further.

Jessy needed to get stabilized before she would be ready to explore how her current symptoms connected to childhood and past traumas. Her first step was to understand what was happening inside her body and how it had adapted to keep her safe. Only then could she begin to develop mechanisms to help herself calm her body's response. This is what so many of my clients come to therapy seeking: emotion regulation and grounding tools to mitigate triggers and overwhelm. Jessy needed these tools in order to feel safer in the world and in her body, so she could enjoy life and feel less dysregulated every day. Even though the world is truly not a safe place for her, as trans people are four times more likely to be assaulted than cisgender people,[1] she understood that it didn't serve her to live in total fight-or-flight mode every day, and the toll it was taking on her body wasn't sustainable.

HOW OUR BODIES KEEP US SAFE

The nervous system is our body's command center. It controls our thoughts, movements, and reactions to the world around us. There are two main branches of the nervous system: (1) the *central nervous system*, which consists of the brain and spinal cord, and (2) the *peripheral nervous system*, a complex system of nerves throughout the body, like the tender veins in a leaf.

Within the peripheral nervous system there are two more branches: the *somatic nervous system* and the *autonomic nervous system*. The somatic nervous system controls our voluntary movements. The autonomic nervous system, which we will focus on in this chapter, controls our bodies' automatic functioning and responses to stimuli. When we experience an unsafe situation or a trigger, it is this system that mobilizes us toward safety, often without our conscious brain knowing that's what we are doing. In fact, our brain often shuts off our critical thinking so we can focus on getting to safety in these moments. When we are triggered and a survival response is activated, we call this a trauma response.

Let's go through a common scenario.

You are at work, on the train, somewhere in public. You experience a subtle or not-so-subtle act that shows someone does not see or believe in your humanity. Maybe you are misgendered, called a racial slur, or find that the place you need to go is not accessible for your body. Your nervous system interprets this as a threat to your life or sense of self—a trigger of past trauma and discrimination—sending your body into survival mode. Our autonomic nervous system is designed to keep us safe at all costs, so it's not going to do a lot of evaluating here. Meaning, even if we are actually safe in the moment, our autonomic nervous system is going to jump into action, reacting below our level of consciousness.

Our body has two autonomic response options to increase our chances of survival.

Option one is the *sympathetic* nervous system response. Our adrenal glands release the stress hormones adrenaline and cortisol, which are responsible for activating the fight-or-flight or the hyperfreeze (freezing with tons of adrenaline in our body) response. Our body invests lots of energy in preparing us to move either toward the threat by fighting back, or away from the threat by fleeing—or freezing in place, hoping to not be seen at all. Our hearts race while the adrenaline courses through our bloodstream, and we may feel our palms sweat and our senses heighten.

Option two, the *parasympathetic* nervous system response, occurs when our brains have determined that it isn't safe to fight back or run away. Our bodies release acetylcholine, a chemical that slows down the heart rate and takes us into the survival responses of submit, attach, or hypofreeze (freeze with little to no stress hormone in our body). We can submit to the threat by seeming to ignore it or by laughing it off. We can attach, which is our people-pleasing or codependent response of needing to stay connected at all costs to the person who has hurt us. This typically occurs when the harm comes from within a major relationship in our life—a parent, a partner, a friend, or a boss. Hypofreezing in place may sound like the hyperfreeze induced by adrenaline, but in this case, we typically feel tired, numb, and dissociated—the sensation of being outside of your own body.

It's important to note that both these nervous systems are not only responsible for survival responses. The parasympathetic nervous system allows us to relax and feel calm, to enter our rest-and-digest state, which is when our body feels safe enough to recharge and to perform some basic functions that get put on hold during stress or trauma. The sympathetic branch, when activated in safe scenarios, is responsible for excitement, motivation, and nervousness over a hot date or a momentous event.

YOUR TURN

When you feel threatened, does your body respond with a sympathetic nervous system response? What triggers you into fight-or-flight mode? When it happens, what do you notice in your body?

What about a parasympathetic nervous system response?

Do you have a default option when triggered or overwhelmed, or does it depend on the scenario? Or do you experience both, and if so, what does that look like for you? Take some time to reflect on how your unique nervous system keeps you safe.

THE ROOTS OF YOUR TRAUMA RESPONSE

Recognizing trauma as the root of people's day-to-day unhappiness or anxiety also helps us to depathologize ourselves and one another. Our culture has some pretty judgmental and problematic beliefs about mental health. When we include trauma in the larger conversation about mental health, we create more compassion and understanding for more people.

One often-overlooked cause of trauma is chronic stress. Jessy certainly suffered from chronic stress. Many of us in the margins do. She also suffered from chronic illness, which is another often-unrecognized source of trauma. Other root causes of trauma arose before we were born—and reside in our genes.

Stress

Most of my clients experience daily stress—worry and mental tension—in their lives, ranging from worry over lack of access to resources, to relationships, to our political and climate reality, to existing in bodies that are seen as less worthy of basic human rights. Our body's neurochemical response to stress is similar to its response to trauma, releasing a flood of adrenaline and cortisol that puts us into fight-or-flight mode or triggers other nervous system responses to perceived danger. Sometimes stress itself is also traumatic, meaning it leaves a lasting impact on our ability to feel safe in the world and connected to others. Stress can limit our ability to get the resources and safety we need in life, even as the lack of resources and safety is the source of stress, creating a vicious cycle.

Stress and trauma can show up in the body not just as the emotional and physical distress of nervous system dysregulation but through chronic pain and illness as well. In no way are chronic pain and illness always trauma related. Yet many of my clients have been told that their chronic illness and pain is "all in their head." As we dig deep into the power of our nervous system and how it keeps us safe, it's important that we also recognize the source of that misunderstanding and how truly dangerous it is.

Though chronic illness can be traumatic and is enormously stressful, the inverse is not necessarily true: that trauma causes chronic illness. This can sometimes be true, yes, but the assumption that unexplained chronic pain has no physical cause is one I see too often in my practice. It's made by doctors who have sent their clients to trauma therapy, writing off their very real pain and illness as psychosomatic. I have seen clients suffer long-term damage to their joints, lose decades of their lives, and disbelieve their own lived experiences because they weren't properly diagnosed. Many illnesses are genetic and are not resolved when someone makes a change to their life, processes their trauma, or reduces stress.

But stress *can* trigger genetic health conditions. And it is vital that we understand what is going on and where chronic illness or pain is coming from, versus chalking it all up to either purely a medical issue or entirely stress and trauma. Our bodies have such a deep, inherent wisdom that it takes curiosity, trust, and attunement to fully understand what it has to tell us. Recognizing how our nervous system tries to keep us safe is key. Whatever we can do to feel safer in the here and now will help our bodies see the safety that is available to us in this moment, and might even allow us to feel more at home in our bodies. We'll explore how Jessy was able to help her body feel safe later in this chapter.

The Trauma in Our Genes

Stress impacts us more deeply when it has occurred for decades in our lives or even intergenerationally. There is a connection between trauma, mental illness, and what we inherit from our ancestors.

Mental health is not all one thing. It is not just trauma, it is not just biology or genetics, and it is not just what we inherit from generations past. I think of it like this: Your ancestors and their trauma are the kindling. Genetics (and inherited traits) is the fuel. And your childhood and traumatic life experiences are the match that sets the fire aflame.

Or, this equation:

Ancestors' Trauma and Stress + Genetics + Life Experiences = Our Mental Health

The trauma that we carry in our genes is a concept I will return to time and time again in this book. Our ancestors' stress and trauma experiences actually alter our gene expression. In our lifetime, these genes are either expressed or not, usually depending on how safe our childhood was and whether we experience trauma in our lives. Stressful and traumatic experiences are often what turn on certain genes for addiction, anxiety, depression, personality disorders, and more. Our ancestors' trauma can lead to a higher likelihood of these genes being expressed even though we didn't experience the trauma firsthand.

This is a book on trauma, but in no way am I saying that all mental illness goes back to personal trauma. Or maybe a better way of understanding this is that humans are incredibly adaptive, and mental illness has become an adaptation our brains and bodies use in our confusing and violent world. Those adaptations get passed on through generations, and our own life experiences of trauma, stress, and oppression turn on genes that express mental illness. We'll look at this more closely in chapter 7.

SYMPTOMS OF TRAUMA

When we experience trauma, our body not only expresses or worsens certain mental illnesses, it also develops adaptations to keep us safe in an unsafe world. These adaptations are known as post-traumatic stress disorder, or PTSD.

PTSD and cPTSD

PTSD is a set of symptoms that describes our brains' and nervous systems' adaptive responses to trauma that endure for more than one month. Studies have found that chronic stress due to oppression triggers those same adaptive responses.[2]

Not everyone who lives through a traumatic incident experiences any or all of the symptoms of PTSD. However, many experience one or more of the following categories of PTSD symptoms:

- Avoidance: avoidance of people, places, or things. Avoiding any reminders of the traumatic event(s).
- Intrusive memories: reexperiencing, nightmares, flashbacks.
- Negative changes in cognition and mood—our bodies' shutdown mode—which includes depression, numbness, hopelessness, negative beliefs about self and the world, guilt, and shame.
- Hyperarousal and hypervigilance: our bodies' fight-or-flight response, which includes anxiety, being watchful or on guard, and an exaggerated startle response.

Historically, PTSD originated as a diagnosis for those who had experienced war trauma and active combat (before the diagnosis, all we had was the term *shell shock*). In the last four decades, thanks to the work of many women, queer people, and/or people of color in the trauma field,[3] it has expanded to include people with any of a myriad of traumatic life experiences, including sexual assault, chronic pain and medical trauma, traumatic loss and grief, abusive relationships, religious and cult abuse, and more.

Complex PTSD (cPTSD) refers to PTSD that results from ongoing, sustained trauma rather than a single incident or shorter period of time. This type of trauma can happen at any point in someone's life but tends to occur in childhood, or in adulthood when someone is in a trauma that occurs over a long period of time, like an abusive relationship.

People with cPTSD have experienced some or all of the following:

- Ongoing, sustained trauma like domestic violence, an abusive relationship, or medical trauma.
- Childhood abuse (sexual, emotional, and/or physical) and neglect, or witnessing abuse and neglect.
- Disrupted caregiving due to mental illness, drug and alcohol addiction, homophobia or transphobia, chronic illness, or the death, incarceration, or separation through immigration or deportation of a caregiver.
- Experiencing structural violence during childhood, such as growing up in poverty, in families and communities impacted by police violence, or with precarious access to necessary life resources including safe housing or food.
- Taking on adult roles in the family in childhood, such as being the emotional parent to a caregiver, raising other siblings due to neglect, needing or being forced to work to support the family early on.
- Religious trauma, such as being raised in an extremist, misogynist, sex negative, homophobic, and transphobic religious environment, which is often fertile grounds for abuse of all kinds.

Symptoms of cPTSD, as with PTSD, include avoidance, reexperiencing, hyperarousal, and difficulty regulating emotions, especially in close relationships. People with cPTSD also experience higher rates of dissociation,[4] which we'll discuss in a moment. For now, it's enough to recognize that dissociation has a range from simply "checking out" of the present moment to fully disengaging from oneself.

Someone with PTSD who had a safe and affirming childhood

has to relearn how to feel safe in the here and now.[5] There is a familiarity with a sense of safety, a baseline to return to. For someone with cPTSD who has never experienced safety in their life, their work after either a traumatic event or the recognition of chronic trauma will be learning how to feel safe and authentic, maybe for the very first time.

Notice that the experiences that may cause cPTSD include "impact of social structures on childhood like growing up in poverty, in families and communities impacted by police violence, or with precarious access to necessary life resources." Countless studies show that the stress of discrimination and microaggressions leaves people experiencing PTSD and cPTSD symptoms.[6] For my clients who grew up in poverty, in abusive homes, in communities ravaged by racism and police violence, and in homophobic and transphobic homes, it can seem impossible to feel safe in the here and now.

If someone experiences abuse and neglect during childhood, they learn as kids that their body isn't theirs, that they have to ignore its signals that something is wrong, and that intimacy isn't safe. They learn that other people can't be trusted and that the world is an unsafe place where bad things can easily happen. Later in life, it is hard to feel connected to their body, to maintain a core sense of self, or to be in close physical relationships that feel safe or authentic. My clients who experienced childhood trauma feel as though they are building a self from scratch in therapy, that their childhood did not give them the chance to fully discover what it is like to be themselves, to be fully human.

Childhood abuse and neglect are some of the most common underlying reasons clients end up in my office but they aren't often consciously aware of this when they seek me out. Recently, I've felt hopeful seeing an uptick in clients who already have and use this language, mentioning cPTSD either as a diagnosis or something they recognize in themselves. It's exciting and empowering to see how our culture is moving toward acknowledging this kind of trauma, and that there is more of a conversation around it in the zeitgeist. We will dig deeper into childhood and attachment theory in chapters 3 and 6.

Dissociation

Anyone with PTSD and cPTSD has experienced dissociation to some degree. Let's explore how our bodies use this trauma response as a technique designed to help us survive.

Dissociation is our body's way of managing overwhelm. It's common among people who have experienced trauma, but it is something we all use from time to time.

We all check out for a bit and give our brain little breaks throughout the day from everything it does for us. It's like when we lose track of time driving and don't remember parts of the trip, a phenomenon sometimes called highway hypnosis. These episodes are on the mild end of the dissociation spectrum.

In the middle range of the spectrum, those of us who have experienced significant trauma and stress can find ourselves using dissociation frequently as a coping strategy. People with PTSD and cPTSD may experience dissociation whenever they feel triggered, but they also might feel dissociated a lot of the time as a way to manage the stress of daily living with PTSD.

People with dissociation can experience two more extreme types: depersonalization or derealization, which we will cover in more depth in chapter 4.

Our capitalist culture actually requires all of us to dissociate to get through the day. I have many clients who say they don't feel human—they feel totally divorced from their bodies, just floating heads working at a computer all day or robots completing the same physical tasks over and over again. Very little about this world brings us back to ourselves, and we have to work and fight too hard to live in the moment. When you add trauma to the mix, it is nearly impossible to feel connected to ourselves and to the present.

Dissociative amnesia, which many people with PTSD and cPTSD experience, is the term for loss of memory for no known medical reason. I hear this frequently from clients: "I just don't really remember my childhood," or "I have the worst memory ever." There is always an adaptive reason for this. If our brains' main goal is to keep us safe, think about how adaptive it is to just forget entire years of our lives if we were being abused or felt unsafe or unloved during that time.

My clients are sometimes aware they use dissociation as a survival resource, and at other times are completely unaware of its role in their protective system. It's important to recognize dissociation as a protective response in all of these ways—from its mildest to its most severe forms.

HONORING THE BODY'S WISDOM

When Jessy came to me with a diagnosis of anxiety and depression, she had also experienced childhood trauma in the form of familial abandonment and estrangement—she grew up as a closeted trans child in a family hostile to the fact that she could not conform to their definition of masculinity. She wanted to feel better on a daily basis and to process the lasting impact of her family's transphobia and rejection. Jessy was also experiencing a lot of stress in her life due to her lack of access to consistent health care and daily experiences of transmisogyny, the intersection of both transphobia and misogyny.

Our first step for Jessy was the stabilization phase of treatment, where we would work together to find ways for her to feel more connected and grounded, as well as determine goals and the scope of our work together. The stabilization phase is also the time when clients can address other ways their body has for coping with stress, unhappiness, or anxiety that might get in the way of feeling more connected, including drug use, alcohol consumption, food restriction or binging, self-harm, dissociation, and more. This type of coping is called survival resourcing. More simply put, we do what we need to survive. We make use of the resources we have, even if they aren't sustainable ones. I will expand on survival resources in chapter 2, and I'll offer creative tools that help us feel more connected to ourselves rather than numbing us out.

Jessy needed to find stabilization first so that she had the capacity both in her nervous system and her life for trauma processing. To figure out what was going on, Jessy filled out a questionnaire, where she named that she was experiencing the following daily symptoms:

Fatigue/low energy
Depressed mood
Tearful or crying spells
Anxiety
Panic
Isolation from others
Chronic pain
Dissociation

I asked her what this looked like for her specifically, and she took me through a recent, and typical, day in her life:

Jessy jolts awake in the morning with a cascade of adrenaline to a loud, piercing noise, her mind soon realizing it's her phone ringing. Her health insurance company is calling to alert her that there was an issue with her paperwork and she no longer has coverage. Jessy takes medication every day for chronic joint pain, and without insurance coverage for it, she not only can't afford it but won't be able to do her job. Jessy is also on hormones, and not having access to them has a variety of impacts on her mental and physical well-being. The stress from this call is already sending signals throughout her body that she is in danger, even though her cognitive brain is telling her she "shouldn't be so dramatic" (the internalized voice of both her parents and our society).

While she waits on hold to see what the issue is, she gets dressed, assessing what outfit she could wear that will invite the least attention from people on the street but still affirm her gender. She takes the anti-inflammatory meds she has left, hoping that they help with the arthritis she can already feel waking up in her joints. Someone from the insurance company she's been transferred to deadnames her (uses the name she was given at birth by her parents instead of her chosen one), sending a sickening feeling deep into her belly. Jessy suddenly feels extremely tired, and yet, still anxious. Her thoughts range from "What's the point?" to various "What if . . . ?" fears about her health, her transition, and her ability to work.

She spends her morning advocating for herself on the phone while applying just a bit of eyeshadow, hands shaking with pain and stress. She heads out the door, already running late, and her stress hormones—cortisol and adrenaline—are raging, like she is preparing for battle. Headphones on so she can't hear any remarks on the train. She commutes for an hour and a half to her job, which involves repetitive work that drains her. Ten hours later, she comes home too depleted to make dinner. Completely exhausted, she gets in bed with her laptop, avoiding texts from friends, and watches TV. She doesn't feel connected to her body. She doesn't feel happy. She doesn't feel like her life is hers. At this point in the day, she doesn't really feel anything at all.

This is the daily reality of so many of us who are burdened by stress, past or ongoing trauma, and the impact of the world on us.

Our bodies have had to adapt, using whatever tools and methods are at hand to keep us safe—from the ones that make us whole to the ones that simply numb us to any sensation at all. In Jessy's case, she utilizes what so many of us do after a long day of overworking: dissociating in front of the TV. This allows her to disconnect from the physical pain and overwhelm she experiences all day.

Jessy and I talked about how anxiety is our sympathetic nervous system trying to mobilize us toward safety. Think about a doe running away from a wolf ready to attack. This is our fight-or-flight response. For Jessy growing up trans in an unsupportive family, and for so many marginalized people, the wolf was everywhere in their childhoods. Unfortunately, the wolf is still everywhere, even though Jessy has gotten away from her family of origin. It is there as she leaves the house, tries to get hormones or surgery approved, or watches other trans women be murdered on the news. But it was Jessy's fight-or-flight response that got her away from her family, and that was lifesaving for her. It keeps her moving through the daily obstacles trans folks deal with in our society. This anxiety response is her body's attempt to keep her safe.

With this framework, we can start to see anxiety, panic, and stress as neurobiological adaptations to stress and trauma. Our body releases stress hormones that mobilize us toward safety, to let us know something isn't right. Our hypervigilance—being watchful or on guard—becomes a protective part of us.

Jessy and I also discussed how depression can be seen as our body's total shutdown mode, our way to not be seen or heard, and therefore safe. It is similar to a reptile freezing or a mammal playing dead. We are here, frozen in shutdown mode, when our bodies have determined our best option is to fully retreat. This looks like depression, dissociation, numbing, oversleeping, checking out. Jessy had to use these responses all the time as a child when it literally wasn't safe to be seen. At home, she received physical and verbal punishment for experimenting with gender or doing anything that was seen as not in alignment with what was expected of her.

Depression is so stigmatized in our overproductive hustle culture, and people whose bodies respond in this way to stress and trauma are seen as weak, lazy, and just not able to pull themselves up by their bootstraps and get over it. Understanding this shutdown as protective helps us grow to love and understand these responses, seeing that they are vital parts of us. This framework helps us feel resilient rather than broken. We can foster love, compassion, and appreciation for the way our bodies and brains have learned to cope and survive.

Before the birth of our first child, my wife found herself in a depression for the first time since she came out. She was gearing up to become a mother, and we were reckoning with the second-parent adoption process we would have to go through so that she could be a legal parent to her own child. She was also trying to balance a full-time job and a dissertation. You would think that her body's response would be anxiety and overwhelm, but the stress was so much that she went into shutdown mode. Her body had determined it would be best if she just powered off, probably trying to conserve some energy before the birth and also to fire the alarm bells that something wasn't okay.

Instead of judging this response, we can get curious about it: Why is my body taking me here? What do I need to do to honor my body's wisdom?

Anxiety and depression are not only nervous system responses—like many other health issues, they can also show up in our genetics. Generalized anxiety disorder (GAD) has a heritability rate of 31.6 percent and depression's heritability rate is 37 percent.[7] While it has recently become popular to give more attention to the connection between stress and trauma and both of these mental health issues, the genetic component cannot be overlooked.[8] Trauma and stress impact the way certain genes are expressed. It is possible that heritable mental illnesses come from our biological lineage, but the conditions of our lives, and our childhoods specifically, activate those genes. Perhaps someone like Jessy has the gene for anxiety and depression, inherited from her parents and generations before them, and her hostile childhood enabled those genes to be expressed.

Studies have shown that PTSD can be experienced by the next generation after a trauma, even if they have not experienced the trauma themselves. One study examined the DNA of mothers who had experienced a traumatic event before becoming pregnant.[9] In some of these cases, changes to the mothers' DNA led to their PTSD symptoms being transmitted to their children, even though they had not been pregnant at the time of the trauma.

So much of what shows up for us in the here and now is from generations past. It's important that we acknowledge and honor all of the ways our ancestors' bodies learned to survive.

I know my anxiety is both genetic—I inherited it from a traumatized lineage of my Ashkenazi Jewish ancestors—and from childhood experiences. I also know that my anxiety has served a real purpose for me in my life in keeping me from harm, as it did my ancestors. When I love and honor this part of my adaptive body, I don't feel as much shame or frustration with it, which ultimately lessens the anxiety. Through years of therapy and making changes to my life that support feeling more regulated, I have become very good at showing my own brain and body that it's safe.

TOOLS FOR STABILIZATION—HOW TO SOOTHE YOUR BODY

Once Jessy understood that the anxiety she experienced on a daily basis was her nervous system on high alert, trying to keep her safe in a world that constantly felt unsafe, we worked on ways of showing her nervous system the safety that does exist in her life. This first step of any healing journey is to learn to feel safe in ways that are sustainable and authentic. While there is no such thing as "bad" coping, there is coping we do in survival mode. I don't shame my clients for utilizing ways of surviving that are deemed unhealthy; I have used many of these methods myself. We always want to honor our body's resiliency, even when it doesn't follow what our society considers acceptable.

Safe Place

The first tool Jessy and I worked on to help her lower her ever-present sense of danger was her Safe Place,[10] a spot she could visit in her mind when she felt triggered or unsafe. On the train, at work, or anytime she felt a threat, she could mentally transport herself to where she felt safe and free and at peace: the queer and trans topless beach in Jacob Riis Park in Queens, New York. When she imagined herself swimming topless with hundreds of other queer and trans people, feeling her body held by her community and the ocean, she would notice her nervous system start to relax. She created an affirmation to go with this Safe Place, which she named Gay Beach: "I am safe, I am loved, it's beautiful to be me."

For anyone who moves through the world feeling generally unsafe, having a Safe Place that acts as a nervous-system anchor is key. While we can't always be at the queer beach, at our grandmother's kitchen table, or in the woods, we can use the Safe Place exercise to tap into the feelings, images, and sensations of somewhere our bodies feel fully welcome and calm.

Now that you've had an introduction to the concept, it's time to find your own Safe Place to use when you need to ground yourself.

YOUR TURN

Safe Place Exercise

Take a few minutes to scan your memory for a place that feels peaceful and calming in your mind's eye. This should be somewhere truly safe and neutral—a place without any relational complication, nothing that will remind you of something hard or sad. Nine times out of ten, people situate their safe space in nature. It might also be their own home, a scenario with beloved animals, a concert or community space, or somewhere relaxing.

Once you have chosen your Safe Place, really notice every detail in this place. Check in with all five senses: What do you see, smell, taste, feel, and hear? If you're in nature, what season is it? Are you alone or are there others around you or nearby? See if you need to bring anything here to make it feel even safer, like a camping cot or tent if you're outside, some cozy blankets if you're indoors—whatever is going to reinforce the calm and safety of this environment you've chosen.

Picture yourself there. How do you imagine yourself in this place? Locate your body in the Safe Place, and start to notice what is happening inside you. How does your body feel checking in with this special place of yours? Take note of what is happening inside. Do you feel calm, connected, at ease? What body sensations tell you that? Is your heart rate slowing down, or do you feel more aware of your body? Do you feel warmth inside your chest?

If you still feel distressed or disconnected, see what it's like to return to that five-sense perception again and keep adding new details to this place. Is there anything else that needs to be here in order for it to feel peaceful?

Now pick a word or phrase to describe this environment. This will be your cue word to instantly bring you to your Safe Place after a trigger or anytime you need to ground yourself. Say this word to yourself a few times silently or out loud. Connect it with the image of this place.

Like Jessy, you can also pick a grounding affirmation or statement that encourages even more safety and connection. Some kind of "I am" statement. If you are struggling to pick one, here are a few:

"I am safe."

"It's okay to be me."

"I am good."

"I am held by the earth/universe/my community."

Creating a TICES Log

We tend to move through the world experiencing triggers and overwhelming emotions and just press on with our day. Our society has little time and space for these feelings, and so keeping a log can help us make time to check in and tend to ourselves.

Jessy kept a weekly log to record her triggers. In it, she noted what the trigger was, what happened in her body, the belief about herself that went along with it, and what she did to cope. She identified in her log that every time she was misgendered or deadnamed, it triggered the traumatizing transphobia from her family of origin and the pain of being forced to grow up and go through puberty in a gender that was not hers. This in turn triggered the belief "It's not safe to be me," which put her nervous system on high alert, causing the physical symptoms of anxiety in her body. Then, later, it would all come crashing down into depression. Now when these triggers come up, she is able to slow things down and say, "I'm triggered," and call to mind her Safe Place. The recognition and validation alone calm her.

A helpful log structure is the TICES log below. TICES stands for Trigger, Image, Cognition (Thoughts), Emotions, and Sensations.[11] Here's Jessy's log as an example.

Trigger: What happened? *Someone on the train loudly asked their friend, "Is that a man?"*

Image: What image came to mind? *Image of my dad telling nine-year-old me I will never be a girl.*

Cognition: What thought or belief was brought up? *That my transition will never be good enough, no one will ever fully see me as a woman.*

Emotion: What were you feeling? *Hopeless and scared.*

Body Sensation: What happened in your body? *First, my heart began racing and I felt a lot of energy in my fists and also in my legs. Then, later, I felt a crash and my body was really heavy.*

How I Coped: What skills and resources did I use to come back to safety? *I went to my Safe Place in my mind's eye, texted another trans girl about what happened, and made a plan to see her and some other friends later tonight. I felt more connected after reaching out.*

YOUR TURN

Create your own TICES log by asking yourself the following questions after you experience a trigger. I suggest actually writing this out either on your notes app on your phone or taking pen to paper later when you can:

Trigger: What was the triggering event or experience that led to me feeling dysregulated?

Image: What image came to mind of a past experience that this experience brought up in the here and now?

Cognition: What negative belief goes along with this image? This is usually a "I am" statement, like "I'm not safe" or "I'm not enough."

Emotion: Now check in with your emotions. How did you feel? What are you feeling now?

Body Sensation: Notice your body: What sensations did you find there? Did you feel heaviness or pain anywhere? Do you still? What did you notice in your throat, heart, gut?

How I Coped: Ask yourself how you coped or how you can cope. What did you do to feel better? Did you reach out to someone? Take a walk? Go to your Safe Place in your mind?

Window of Tolerance

The next idea I introduced Jessy to is the window of tolerance (WOT).[12] This is a state of being in which life seems manageable and you feel calm and alert. When we experience stress, trauma, oppression, or instability as a child, the window of what we can tolerate emotionally as an adult may be small. Because Jessy had experienced familial rejection trauma as a child and young adult, triggers, emotions, and stimuli could bring her out of what felt tolerable very quickly. Her window of tolerance was very narrow.

When we aren't taught self-regulation from our caregivers and instead learn to numb ourselves rather than feel, it is hard to stay within our window of tolerance. A trigger, threat, or overwhelming emotion takes us into survival mode. Some of us go *above* our window into overwhelm and some of us go *below* our window into shutdown mode. Some of us do one or the other depending on the context. For Jessy, when she was triggered in public, she experienced what is called hyperarousal. Her sympathetic nervous system responded by feeling anxious and her fight-or-flight response kicked in. She felt that she was in an intolerable place (outside her window of tolerance), and her body wanted to get her out of danger now.

HYPERAROUSED

Anxious • Angry • Fight or Flight

WINDOW OF TOLERANCE

Grounded • Calm • Connected

HYPOAROUSED

Depressed • Disassociated • Numb

For someone else, feeling triggered might make them experience hypoarousal. Their parasympathetic nervous system activates, and they might feel exhausted. In some cases, they might check out mentally and even view themselves from outside their bodies (dissociation).

When we are within our windows of tolerance, we feel comfortable—our nervous systems are neither hyper- nor hypoaroused, our heart rates are steady, and we are able to feel present and safe in the here and now.

Expanding that window of tolerance is an essential part of stabilization in trauma treatment. When we are within this window we can feel, connect and relate, and tolerate what life has thrown our way. An exercise like imagining our Safe Place brings us home in our bodies to our window of tolerance. Inside our window of tolerance is where real change happens in therapy, which is why it's so important to go slow and establish an understanding of what it feels like to be there. If we skip stabilization and jump right into processing, then we can overwhelm our nervous system, sending it into fight, flight, or total shutdown, which makes it hard for any real change to occur. So many of us don't know what our window of tolerance is because we've never asked ourselves to discover it.

YOUR TURN

Finding Your Window of Tolerance

Float back in your memory to a time when you were grounded, at peace, and connected to your body and the world around you. You can use a memory from earlier in the book from the Your Turn exercise about tracking your body's sensations. In the middle of a sheet of paper, write a name for this memory. You could call it something like "My son's tenth birthday" or "Naked at the beach." This is your window-of-tolerance memory. Write down some words around the name of the memory. How did you feel physically? How did you feel emotionally? Now, at the top of the piece of paper, write down the name of a memory where you were in fight or flight—you were angry, irritable, anxious, or scared. This is your hyperaroused-state memory. Maybe it's called "Yelling at a cop at the protest" or "Being misgendered at the doctor's office." Write down some descriptor words for this state as well. At the bottom of your piece of paper, write down the name of a memory associated with your hypoaroused state—a time when you felt shut down, depressed, dissociated, numb, dead inside. It might be called "Day after the election" or "After I got fired." What did you feel emotionally and physically when this happened? Write down some descriptor words here as well.

Now look at your piece of paper. You have charted your nervous system. Your work when you feel hyper- or hypoaroused is to notice the sensations in your body and the feelings that are similar to these memory examples. From here, you can figure out what you need to come back into your window-of-tolerance state.

Finding Compassion, Freedom, and Community Inside Yourself

Jessy could return to her window of tolerance by going to her Safe Place. She had also already been doing a lot on her own to get here. She had experienced ways of coming back to herself through connection with friends and bodily expression, including her transition, swimming naked in the ocean at the queer beach, and having sex that felt authentic and aligned with her desires. Jessy had brought herself back into her window and her body through compassion, freedom, and community. And it was vital that we acknowledge and honor her intuitive action together. These core experiences of trauma healing tend to be what lead us back within our window of tolerance: compassion, freedom, and community. These three words can help you to come back to yourself time and again.

YOUR TURN

Pick a few memories of times you felt self-compassion, connected to others in community, and freedom in your body. These experiences can function as anchors.

Give each memory a name like "Nature walk" or "Lesbian sex party" that can bring you back to that experience in your mind's eye. Just like with Safe Place, try to recall details that

> involve your five-sense experience of this memory to really live inside of it. Even when compassion, freedom, and community are not readily available to us in the moment, we can return to a time in our minds where we felt embodied and connected.

BRINGING IT ALL TOGETHER

Our nervous system is designed to adapt and keep us from harm. There is much we can do to help ourselves understand why we respond to stress and trauma the way we do, to not pathologize those responses. When we come to therapy or healing with curiosity about our bodies' responses instead of judgment, there is much more space to learn and grow. Take some time to write down a few pieces of information from this chapter that you want to take with you. Consider them tools that can guide you on your path of depathologizing your wildly adaptive body's protective nervous system. Are there any old ways of thinking about mental health that you want to leave behind?

In the next chapter, we'll take a deeper dive into the workings of our wonderfully flexible, protective, and resilient brains.

CHAPTER 2

How Our Brains Respond to Trauma

In a recent session, my client Vee said to me: "Everything is safe now. I have a home, a wife, a baby on the way, but my brain can't stop scanning for danger. I am always waiting for something bad to happen. I can't even enjoy my own life."

As we learned in the previous chapter, our nervous system interprets the information around us and, without our conscious awareness, determines whether we are safe or in danger. If it determines we are in danger, it activates our survival responses to get us to safety as quickly as possible. Vee's nervous system had stayed on high alert after experiencing lifelong oppression-based trauma. It was keeping them from seeing the safety their life now had to offer.

When something reminded Vee of the past, suddenly the safe present didn't feel so safe. This makes sense, especially for someone like Vee, who is nonbinary and Black, and who has experienced the traumas of white supremacy, religious trauma, and a lifetime of rejection within their family of origin.

Even when it is safe, getting close to other humans and building a life with a partner or within a community is hard. We all experience this. Our brain and body, remembering past traumatic experiences, may tell us to run when we are perfectly safe. How and why do they do this? And what about when life truly isn't safe? What if there is no safe "now" to come back to?

In this chapter, we'll explore our flexible, protective, and resilient brains. You'll learn how your brain keeps you safe through its own survival mode, a mode you ultimately have control over through mindfulness and neuroplasticity. And we'll explore different theories that will help you come into a fuller understanding of how we process trauma, especially oppression-based trauma.

I'll show you how your brain can grow and change through *mismatches*—the term that we in the trauma therapy field use for experiences that don't line up with what our brain thinks is going to happen—which can actually reroute your neural pathways to alter your beliefs about yourself. The three core branches of healing—compassion, freedom, and community—are all areas where we can implement mismatches. A mismatch can be a safe and loving relationship after an abusive one, a community that embraces you after you've experienced rejection, or a therapist with whom you feel held and seen after a childhood of neglect.

You'll also get to know Sam in the pages below. A gay man who used drugs and alcohol to help him deal with trauma, Sam learned to create new pathways in his brain through Alcoholics Anonymous (AA), mindfulness practices, and a trauma therapy technique to process painful memories called EMDR, which you'll learn all about.

Those of us who, like Vee, suffered rejection and abuse as children are unable to feel safe in the here and now as adults. I'll share with you the tools that helped Vee create mismatches and assure their mind and body that they can find safety within. I'll also teach you the Daily Mismatch Ritual and introduce the grounding practice of Anchor Objects, and together we can practice an exercise I call Container for storing your traumatic memories.

With this chapter, you'll learn to reroute your brain's neural pathways to support your trauma healing.

YOUR BRAIN ON TRAUMA AND STRESS

Learning how our brain stores traumatic memories is the first step in understanding how we can use its flexibility to heal. Our brain and spinal cord—our central nervous system—act as our command center. The nerves that branch off our spinal cord and into the rest of our bodies is the peripheral nervous system, which you got to know intimately in the last chapter.

For the sake of understanding trauma and how your brain adapts, think of your brain as a complex series of pathways known as neural networks. When neural networks serve you well—that is, keep you safe—your brain remembers. When you successfully use a survival response, your brain recalls that pattern of connections and uses it again when triggered. It will say, "Ah yes, I recognize this, I know what to do here." For example, if you have used flight to get through a past traumatic experience, when you get overwhelmed, your nervous system will default to that pattern.

Memory is not stored in your brain like a computer file. Memory *is* your neural networks reconstructing past information in the present. Essentially, with traumatic memories, you're not remembering them; you're reliving them.[1]

In my early twenties, I was in an unhealthy, unsafe relationship. I finally ended that relationship with a lot of help from my community and a supportive therapist. But afterward, every time I saw someone with long blonde hair, my brain recalled information from the past. I had built neural pathways associating long blonde hair with danger. Have you ever thought you saw someone familiar on the street and it wasn't them? That is your brain making its best guess when presented with similar characteristics to someone in your life. For my brain, long blonde hair = danger. And my heart would start racing even though that blonde person on the street was a stranger.

What was really going on? To start, let's get to know the regions of your brain responsible for creating and holding memory: the medial prefrontal cortex, the hippocampus, the amygdala, and Broca's area.

Medial Prefrontal Cortex (mPFC)

The medial prefrontal cortex (mPFC) sits at the front of your brain. It's an area where many neural pathways converge and lots of information is processed. If your brain's networks were trails in a park, your mPFC would be a popular destination on the hike, with lots of activity and intersecting pathways. Or a major airport, with passengers making connecting flights there. The mPFC is associated with emotion regulation, cognition, and the ability to socialize. Studies show that stress actually decreases neural network branching in the mPFC,[2] as if some of those trails that lead to that popular destination on the hike get completely washed out. Think about it: If the mPFC is involved in emotion regulation, and you are someone who has experienced a lifetime of trauma, of *course* it's hard to regulate your emotions, or be social, or form connections. Think about how difficult it is to focus when you are stressed or overwhelmed. Imagine if you were *always* stressed or overwhelmed. Research shows that when survivors are cued with upsetting words related to their trauma, there is decreased blood flow to the mPFC.[3]

The Hippocampus, Amygdala, and Broca's Area

The hippocampus is a thin band shaped like a seahorse near the center of your brain. It's associated with memory. Many trauma survivors struggle to remember traumatic incidents. People who have stressful childhoods frequently don't remember entire years. This is because stress and trauma literally damage neurons in the hippocampus.[4]

Then there's your little almond-shaped amygdala. Small but mighty, it's your brain's fire alarm. It's associated with sparking the fight-or-flight response and survival decision-making. Research has shown that trauma leads to an overactive amygdala and an underactive mPFC.[5] At some point in your life, you've probably lived somewhere with a sensitive smoke detector. Trauma makes our amygdala act like that piercing siren that goes off when you're just trying to make a grilled cheese sandwich. Your amygdala screams, telling you "It's unsafe! Get to safety now!" and cues your body to release stress hormones that mobilize you into fight or flight. A trigger (like seeing someone who looks like someone who caused you trauma) can cause your amygdala to sound the alarm, while your mPFC—which should be engaged and talking you out of a sense of panic—hides under the bed.

The part of your brain known as Broca's area is in the left frontal lobe. It's associated with language and speech—as in, putting thoughts, feelings, and memories into words. After trauma there is, again, increased amygdala function and (yep, you guessed it!) *decreased* function of Broca's area.[6] Have you ever felt like there are no words for the pain or for a traumatic experience? This is why. (A client of mine likes to say, "My Broca's area is broke!")

For those of us who have dealt with the very real impact of chronic illness, poverty, white supremacy, and/or homophobia or transphobia all our lives, our brains have literally formed under stress.

If you find it depressing to learn about the impact of trauma on your brain, hang on. We're about to get to the hopeful part. And there really is a hopeful part. The good news is that our brains are incredibly flexible, adaptive, and capable of healing.

HOW OUR BRAINS REWIRE AND HEAL

We *can* heal from trauma, it just takes a lot of new, different experiences, thoughts, and feelings repeated over and over. We heal through anything that gives us that new and transformative experience of a *mismatch*.[7] When given a mismatched experience, our brain will rewire itself—imagine forging a new trail—to make new associations. We will cover a number of ways to rewire your brain away from well-worn pathways created by trauma and stress and toward new pathways created by compassion, community, and freedom.

For me, thanks to trauma therapy and years of being in a safe, healthy relationship, I haven't mistaken a blonde, long-haired person for my ex-girlfriend in years. My brain no longer equates long blonde hair with danger. Our brains really can and do rewire and heal themselves when we have new experiences. Triggers can fade into the distance as we establish a sense of safety in the here and now.

Exactly how the brain rewires and heals is thanks to its remarkable *neuroplasticity*—the ability to change based on experience. This ability to change is how we learn anything and everything—from when to feel afraid to how to feel safe.

Neuroplasticity

In the past, neuroscience theorized that our brains were like cement and that once a neural pathway had been created, it could never be undone. But we now know the opposite is true. The well-established pathways in our brain are like boot prints on a popular hiking trail—the more times a trail is walked the wider and more densely packed it becomes. Maybe you've heard the phrase made famous by Canadian psychologist Donald Hebb: "Neurons that fire together, wire together"? Rerouting that trail in the woods results in a new trail, with the old one becoming overgrown with disuse. The brain actually wants to grow and change.

When we strengthen neural pathways, it's called tuning. We tune through repeated experiences or activities. Studies have shown it takes an average of sixty-six days to form a habit.[8] Actions repeated over and over again lead to tuning neural networks, making them stronger and faster.

When a pathway dies out from disuse, we call that pruning. Pruning can be thought of in both a depressing way and a really hopeful way. We are born with twice as many neural connections as we will have as adults. If we grow up in environments with caregivers who aren't able to meet our basic or emotional needs, think about which networks die and which ones are strengthened (more on that in the next chapter on attachment). The hopeful side of how neural networks prune is that we can abandon networks that don't serve us, and they will die off.

Tuning and Pruning Through Mismatches

My client Sam grew up in a home where he learned to cope with stress by using drugs and alcohol. His grandparents and parents had learned to cope with the daily traumas of poverty by drinking and using drugs. Research has shown that not only can addiction genes be passed down, but our own unique genetic code can also include or lack markers that determine how we respond to drugs and alcohol. Remarkably, there are genes that are related to the type of relationship we have to drinking.[9] In the nature versus nurture equation, Sam's addiction had both going for it: nature from genes, and nurture from watching his family use drugs and alcohol to cope. Sam's chosen adult community also tended to use drugs and alcohol to excess. The LGBTQ+ community is twice as likely as heterosexual people to experience alcoholism. Queer and trans youth are almost twice as likely to try and use hard drugs as their heterosexual cis peers.[10]

Sam discovered that drugs gave him what is called a false window of tolerance, which meant that he felt better right away, but his nervous system and brain weren't truly experiencing safety, and the effect only lasted for so long. When Sam experienced a trigger or an overwhelming feeling, his brain had a well-worn path of turning to drugs and alcohol to feel relief. As we have learned, when we are triggered, our body goes into survival mode and our nervous system is going to do whatever it can to get us to safety.

I worked with Sam to develop more awareness, or mindfulness, during a trigger. For Sam, mindfulness came in the form of praying and meditation, skills he picked up in his twelve-step recovery program. Breathing, praying, and talking to his higher power all expanded his window of tolerance and soothed his amygdala when the alarm went off. Using his mindfulness practices, he was able to notice what was happening in his body, in his nervous system, in his brain. When he experienced any trigger for using drugs or drinking, he noticed that his body filled up with energy, that he was desperate for substances to release that energy and wanted to "have some fun." The young, teenage part of himself had come to associate drinking and drugs with being wild and free, something he was never actually able to feel as a child or teen.

Sam worked an incredibly physically and emotionally demanding food industry job. The staff of the restaurant reminded him of his homelife growing up: dysfunctional, unboundaried, stressed out all the time. It didn't help that the staff joked, "We're all family here." The entire crew would go out to a bar after work to drink, do drugs, and "bond."

After one particularly chaotic shift, Sam felt like he was right back in his childhood all over again and found himself scanning the bar for his dealer because that overwhelming feeling had transformed into a craving for drugs. But after a moment, he took a deep breath and noticed how he had been triggered at work all night long and was now searching for a release. With this awareness, he was able to make a conscious choice—one that aligned with his values—instead of a knee-jerk reaction. He activated the new neural networks that he'd developed through therapy and AA. Instead of reaching for drugs and alcohol, Sam began praying. He closed his eyes and spoke to his higher power. Then he called his sponsor—essentially co-regulating, which we'll discuss in the next chapter. If those two practices had not been enough, Sam had a third trick up his sleeve. He could look online for a queer and trans AA or Narcotics Anonymous (NA) meeting to attend in person or virtually, which are available at all hours of the day and night.

Every time Sam is triggered and chooses not to take the old path of substance use, when he instead takes the path of self-compassion using meditation and prayer, seeks out community such as his recovery community, and experiences freedom from his old choices, he reinforces the mismatch with his early response to trauma. As he prunes his old path of addiction, it continues to wither, and as he tunes his new paths of compassion, community, and freedom, those strengthen. While he still experiences cravings, meaning those pathways and genetic predispositions are still there, he has built powerful enough neural networks that allow him to slow down and choose a different path.

Pathways worn deep in childhood served us for so long, keeping us safe through childhood and subsequent trauma and stress, but they ultimately may not allow us to be fully at home with ourselves and the world. As Sam's story shows, we can rewire our brains away from the old, well-worn paths of operating in survival mode, whether the old ways mean numbing ourselves, people pleasing, dissociating from our bodies, or not being our authentic selves. We can steer ourselves toward experiencing compassion, freedom, and community. We can build new trails and do the hard work of clearing away the brush and spiderwebs in the untouched forests of our minds.

There are many ways you can help your brain restructure, taking advantage of its neuroplasticity, including therapy. One such method, practiced with a therapist trained in this healing technique, is known as Eye Movement Desensitization and Reprocessing (EMDR).*

PROCESSING TRAUMA USING EMDR

While trauma blocks your brain's highly adaptive healing process, some types of therapy that focus on trauma processing can *unblock* it. As we learned earlier in the chapter, our brain doesn't store memories like a computer or an old file cabinet; it actually reconstructs memories through neural activity given past information it deems relevant in the here and now. EMDR is one technique that can unblock your brain's healing process.

Treatments like EMDR use the mindful "noticing brain" to process trauma instead of the "thinking brain" that we use when we tell our story in talk therapy, for example. Using the noticing brain means incorporating feelings, body sensations, and the beliefs we hold about ourselves and the world into therapy. While there is great benefit in talk therapy, treatments that incorporate the body, using dual attention awareness—both mind and body stimulation—like EMDR, can be even more effective for specifically treating trauma.

*EMDR is powerful and should only ever be used by a licensed therapist who has received training approved by the EMDR International Association. To find a therapist in your area, you can go to EMDRIA.org.

In an EMDR session, clients are asked to think of a snapshot image of a traumatic experience—called a target—and to identify the feelings this target image brings up in their body, the emotions they're feeling, and a negative belief they hold about themselves as a result of that experience. The therapist might then ask the client to focus on eye movements (the *EM* of EMDR), which can look like following a moving light that goes left and right. Or the bilateral stimulation (BLS) might be tapping the right side and then the left side of the body, or holding buzzers that vibrate in one hand and then the other, or hearing a sound in the right ear, then the left, and so on—while at the same time thinking about the image of the traumatic memory they are working with.

Repeating this process of thinking of the target image while your body is also experiencing bilateral sensations is part of the desensitization part of EMDR. Clients are anchored in the present moment by the BLS while they work through trauma with the therapist's guidance, making the trauma seem less overwhelming than it would be if they were simply verbally processing a memory. This process also gets the body involved to somatically process the story. Not everyone feels overwhelmed when processing trauma—they can actually feel disconnected and dissociated, as if telling a story that happened to someone else. BLS assists with this, too, helping clients to connect with their body during trauma processing, instead of dissociating from it.

Imagine you're the client and I ask you to let your eyes follow the moving light of a light bar (an EMDR tool that is a long horizontal column that a blue light travels back and forth along—each movement back and forth is called a "set"). Your target, or traumatic memory, is held in well-worn networks in your brain. Every time you think of it while your eyes follow the light back and forth and feel less distress, you are building *new adaptive networks* around this memory. As you bring up your target and your eyes follow the light, I invite you to follow the channels of associations in your mind, and as you process this memory under these new circumstances, you begin to make new associations with the target. The original belief associated with that target might be "I'm not safe," which may become "I survived" instead. Emotions of anger and shame associated with that target might instead become resilience and compassion. Once you have completed this part of the therapy, you will have built new associations and beliefs around the trauma. These new adaptive networks are a result of the *R* in EMDR: reprocessing.

After EMDR treatment—which can encompass one session or twenty per target, depending on the client—when a trigger arises, that memory snapshot will be associated with the breakthroughs and triumphs they made during processing, or it will be simply less distressing. I say to clients all the time, "This never has to be your favorite memory, but it should no longer be highly triggering once we are done processing."

In our EMDR sessions, my client Sam wanted to work on feeling less triggered at work. He chose as his target one extreme experience that haunted him and contributed to his stress and desire to use drugs as an adult. As a child, Sam was the caretaker of his mother, who abused drugs and alcohol. This defined his entire childhood. Sam never got to be a kid; his earliest memory is of microwaving dinner for his hungover mother. When Sam was ten, his mother fell asleep while drunk and smoking a cigarette. He awoke to the apartment on fire. This didn't wake his intoxicated mother, who he managed to drag out of the apartment to safety. His childhood was full of traumatic experiences from living with an incapable parent who was struggling with addiction, but this experience was a peak for his trauma.

Like any restaurant kitchen, the one where Sam worked had many open flames, which were highly triggering for him. And, because it was the service industry, everyone smoked, which was also super activating for him. He wanted to process the terrible memory of having to rescue his mother from the fire so he could be less activated by these triggers and feel a little calmer at work, which would aid his own recovery efforts. Here is how we set up Sam's EMDR target:

Image: Dragging my mom out of the apartment

Negative Belief: I have to be vigilant

Positive Belief: It's not all on me

Emotions: Anxiety, sadness, fear

Body Sensations: Hands shaking, heart racing

Here is what processing this target memory looked like: First, Sam noticed a lot of distress in his body. He began experiencing fight-or-flight responses that were similar to the sensations and messages he felt when his home caught fire. His heart would race, he would feel a ton of energy in his legs and a strong desire to leave the environment he was in, and his mouth would go dry. This is what tends to happen during an EMDR session: The distress ramps up, reaches a peak, and sometimes requires grounding in the safe space of the therapy office. Along the way, Sam noticed snapshots of the traumatic memory—other details he had shoved away for decades, not wanting to revisit them. In the safety of the office, now was the time to look through them, all while experiencing nervous system regulation from the BLS and grounding therapeutic relationship. Other memories can come up during this process, and those are processed too.

After ten EMDR sessions, Sam was able to be in the kitchen at work and not feel extremely triggered. He reported that when he thought of the memory, he saw it as more black-and-white and less vivid. Sam also felt more able to connect to his adult self at work, instead of feeling like a scared little kid who has to be an adult.

My client Vee's number one goal was to feel safer in their daily life, or at least "safe enough," compared to their childhood. Vee wanted to be able to teach hold the belief that even while living under the constant threat and unsafety of white supremacy and homopobia and transphobia as a Black nonbinary person, there *was* a way to feel safe at home with the loving family they had worked so hard to create. Since so much of their trauma occurred within their home as a child, the idea of "home" itself could be triggering, even though *now* was so different from *then*.

The target memory we worked with in our EMDR sessions was one particular experience that made it feel impossible for Vee to experience safety at home. It was of the afternoon when Vee returned home from high school and was ambushed in the living room by the pastor and members of their parents' evangelical church. An intervention had been planned to "save" Vee from "the Devil." Vee's emerging gender nonconformity and queerness had been seen as an abomination, which was more fuel on the fire for their already-violent father who needed little excuse to harm them. They fled before the "exorcism" began, but they never returned home, moving in with their girlfriend and her affirming and safe mother. This particular event stood out as an extreme traumatic experience and haunted Vee. It marked the beginning of their estrangement from their family of origin.

Here is how we set up Vee's EMDR target:

Image: Walking into the living room after school and seeing my family, pastor, and church community sitting there waiting for me

Negative Belief: I'm not safe/It's not safe to be me

Positive Belief: I am safe/It's safe to be me now

Emotions: Fear, shame, anger

Body Sensations: Sick to my stomach

During our processing work, Vee was invited to think of the memory itself and those words "I'm not safe" while following the back-and-forth movement of a light bar with their eyes. After thirty sets, I stopped the light and I asked them what images, thoughts, body sensations, and emotions they noticed. We repeated this process.

What gets processed here is any dysfunctional information that was stored during trauma, which was our brain's way to try to keep us safe after trauma.

In our desensitizing phase of our work with this target, Vee processed the negative belief it instilled in them (I'm not safe), the emotions (anger, shame), and the body sensations it still brought up (sick to my stomach). Once the target image was no longer highly distressing, Vee was able to work on reprocessing. During reprocessing, Vee would consciously think of the statement "I am safe" while distracted by the BLS. Gradually, Vee's brain was able to take in and process that they were no longer a child, stuck in their unsafe childhood home.

Vee reported feeling safer at home after this target was completed (which took about ten sessions). They told me, "I feel like that chapter of my life has a beginning, middle, and end now. I know it happened to me, but it doesn't feel like it is still happening anymore."

EMDR therapy is one way to encourage old neural networks to die off and to pave the way for new ones to emerge. But we can also learn to find safety outside of the therapy office. And we can experience this sense of safety through compassion, community, and freedom.

HOW TO FEEL SAFE IN A TIME OF PERPETUAL DANGER

Those of us at the margins not only are triggered when we are reminded of the unsafe past—many of us actually experience *real* unsafety all the time in the present. In our modern world, we contend with climate collapse, fascism, and living in a white supremacist, ableist, homophobic, and transphobic society. Our brain often *correctly* perceives an abstract threat because danger really is all around us. So how do we honor that reality while also telling our bodies that we are safe when we need to soothe our nervous systems?

As a queer person of color, Vee often felt physically unsafe just walking down the street. Additionally, as is the reality for so many Americans, Vee heard gunshots in their neighborhood on a regular basis. Inside their home, they were safe *enough*. But Vee's childhood with a violent father taught them to expect danger within the walls of their home as well as outside it. Was Vee completely, 100 percent safe outside their home now? No. Were they "safe enough" compared to what childhood was like? Yes. They were "safe enough" in the sense that they had an emotionally and physically safe relationship, consistent housing, and access to what they need.

How could Vee tell their body and brain what they consciously knew to be true? The answer was through deliberate practices that would help establish mismatches: a Daily Mismatch Ritual, repetition, and Anchor Objects.

Daily Mismatch Ritual—the Safe-Enough Protocol

If you are feeling unsafe and are trying to calm your brain, you can try this technique.

Scan your environment for safety or danger. Ask yourself the question "Am I actually safe in this moment?" You may find the answer to be *yes*! Yes, you are safe in your current home, relationship, and community. What you are feeling is a trigger linked to a time in your life when your home or family or relationship or circumstance was not safe. If this is the case, you can then create a grounding statement such as "This is just a memory" or "This is just a trigger, reminding me of the past."

What if the answer to the question is *no*? What if you scan the environment and find that you aren't actually safe?

If that's the case, you should ask yourself, "What do I need to feel safe *enough*?" The "enough" question honors the truth that being fully safe may not be an option.

Vee began to practice a daily ritual to help them really take in the mismatch between the safety of their current life and their history, but also to acknowledge the fact that they currently lived in a neighborhood with gun violence. Every day, Vee spent sixty seconds walking through their home, mindfully taking in their surroundings. They would take in the art on the walls they had collected over the years that celebrated queerness; their big, cozy bed they shared with their loving wife; every little plant and decorative pillow. They observed and appreciated the lack of religious material in the home. How no doors had holes punched through them. Vee chose an affirmation to repeat silently while performing this ritual: the words "It is safe to be me." Every single time Vee walked through their home repeating their new belief, the pathways in their brain that sent them into a survival response whenever they heard a loud noise or a gunshot off in the distance weakened. They gradually became able to hold that belief in their safety, to trust that the loud noise in the distance wasn't coming from inside their home like it had when Vee was a child. It wasn't their dad's violence toward them or his family. It was safe to be Vee in their home. Their life now was a mismatch to their childhood. Every walk through the house tuned, or created, new pathways of safety in the here and now and pruned ones associated with the survival responses Vee had needed in childhood.

The Power of Repetition

Vee's Mismatch Ritual worked to create new neural pathways because they performed it every time they entered their home. Practice, practice, practice. It's the secret ingredient to learning anything new.

My client Sam, in addition to our weekly sessions, went to an AA or NA meeting every day. If you're not familiar with twelve-step programs, repetition is key to their success. When you begin a twelve-step program, you are advised to do ninety meetings in ninety days. This builds those much-needed pathways of sobriety quickly. And in each meeting, the same rituals occur. The AA preamble is read. The Serenity Prayer is recited. Everyone introduces themselves as alcoholics: "I'm Andrea and I'm an alcoholic." And everyone says, "Hello, Andrea!" A reading is done from the AA literature. At the end there is a moment of silence for any alcoholics who are not there that day, with the Serenity Prayer again to close the meeting. Think about how much repetition this is! Growing up, Sam's brain had formed around the idea of alcohol and drug use being the normal ways of dealing with stress and big feelings. The repetition of AA meetings helped his brain make new connections about the damage drugs and alcohol cause and helped him develop tools for emotion regulation that don't involve using. Many people who struggle with addiction struggle with giving up control, which is what the Serenity Prayer is all about: *God/Goddess/Earth/Higher Power, grant me the serenity to accept the things I cannot change, the courage to change the things I can, and the wisdom to know the difference.*

Going to therapy is also a form of repetition, regardless of the type of therapy. Just meeting with a compassionate person on a regular basis establishes new pathways and prunes old ones.

Anchor Objects

Sometimes we need a physical object to hold or touch or imagine to provide ourselves with that mismatch, assuring ourselves that we are "safe enough." In graduate school I worked with a queer and trans client who was unhoused. For her, home had been unsafe as a child, and now she squatted where she could in New York City. In a session one day, we dumped out her backpack, paying close attention to every object she owned. Which objects made her body feel safe? We landed on the following: neon pink lipstick. No matter how scary or uncertain her life was, she always felt embodied when she put on her lipstick. It was an *Anchor Object*; it brought her back to herself. It represented self-compassion. The next item: a photo of her friends. While she didn't have a consistent home, she did have a group of other young queer and trans folks who she squatted with in an abandoned warehouse. When she looked at a photo of all of them, she felt belonging and didn't feel so scared and alone. They were her community. And the last object? Her bike chain and lock. They reminded her of her bike, her most important object in the world, and the freedom she felt knowing she could get herself anywhere she needed to be, at any moment. She also knew she could use her lock and chain in self-defense if need be.

When she mindfully ran her hands over these objects, they anchored her. She was able to be "safe enough." Each time she felt self-compassion, community, and freedom, it served as a mismatch to the networks in her brain that had been wired for danger, worn smooth by a lifetime of oppression-based trauma and violence. Each time she was able to calm herself by touching or imagining her Anchor Objects, she pruned old pathways and tuned new ones that helped her believe and feel she was "safe enough."

Container

Another grounding practice that is core to my work is Container. I ask clients to picture in their mind's eye a real or imagined box or a place they can safely store overwhelming feelings, fears, memories, and anxieties. My Container is a real box I have in my home, a vintage floral makeup case. It lives on a shelf in my linen closet and holds some reminders of my party days of the past (glitter, purple lipstick, fake eyelashes). When I experience a trigger, I imagine pulling out that box, putting the upsetting image or feeling or sensation into it, closing the lid, shoving it to the back of a shelf, and closing the closet door. I play out, in my mind's eye, walking away from it. I might also imagine the memory or the trigger as a Polaroid. I imagine putting the photo away in my old makeup box for safekeeping, storing it away where it belongs. Then, if needed, I can process that memory with my therapist or journal about it at a later time when I feel safe.

Container is a trauma-regulation tool. When you give yourself distance from your triggering images, this creates a mismatch—it gives you permission to let that image or memory go for now. It can tune new pathways in the brain and prune the ones that make you feel triggered all the time. Container works well with Safe Place, which you learned about in chapter 1. Your traumatic memories can be put away in your Container, and you can imagine that you yourself have returned to the safety of your Safe Place.

YOUR TURN

Intentionally creating a mismatch takes a bit of preparation and thought. You're going to create your own Mismatch Ritual. This can be a "safe enough" ritual like the one Vee created, some kind of prayer from your recovery or healing journey like Sam's, or reviewing your Anchor Objects like the client I worked with who was unhoused. It can be a Container exercise, similar to the way I think about the box I have in my home. Or it can be something new that is especially meaningful to you. Scan your brain for something you just want to be different in your life, some old belief or trauma response that you would love some distance from.

Now do what we call in EMDR therapy a floatback. Look back at your memories and ask yourself: Where does this negative belief come from? What earlier life experience or experiences led to this being a well-used neural pathway? Take some time to identify and then examine this memory and how it led to this trigger, negative belief, or issue in your life.

Now let's find your "in" to this pathway. What negative belief is it telling you? These are usually:

- I'm/It's not safe
- I'm not enough
- I am bad
- It's not okay to be me
- I have to be perfect
- I can't handle it

Another way to think of this is: What would be a mismatched experience, something that would help you learn that the opposite is true? If this feels impossible, choose something a little smaller to work with, something more tangible for now.

Whatever you choose, the Mismatch Ritual doesn't have to be a big commitment of time or energy, and it can even be something you are already doing but just draw more mindfulness to. Sixty seconds every day is enough. The most important aspect is not how much time you devote to it each day. The most important thing is repetition, which tunes and prunes the pathways. Of course, you can make a bigger commitment to spend more time on this if that is what you desire.

What will your new ritual to create a mismatch be? What is your commitment to yourself to get your brain a new experience so it can tune and prune? Find some more examples of Daily Mismatch Rituals below:

- Spend time with an animal companion. Take in how safe your nervous system feels with them.
- Notice that you are an adult and not a child. Take in that you reside inside of an adult body.
- Say today's date: Help your brain see that today is not the past.

BRINGING IT ALL TOGETHER

Your wonderfully resilient brain stores trauma deep within its neural pathways. When you are triggered or feel unsafe, your brain sounds the alarm and your nervous system sends you into a trauma response. But you can help your brain learn new ways to think about triggers by creating your own mismatch experiences. You can prune old pathways that are locked in old beliefs and thoughts and feelings telling you that you are unsafe, and tune or create new pathways that reflect positive beliefs, thoughts, and feelings that promote healing.

Mismatches can occur through therapy, including the EMDR modality, through twelve-step programs like AA, through community, in safe and loving relationships, and through your relationship to yourself. With experiences where you feel self-compassion and freedom—through creativity, being out in nature, and even right now, reading this book—you are creating or strengthening adaptive pathways in your brain and abandoning old ones. What you're doing with the Daily Mismatch Ritual, Anchor Objects, Container, and Safe Place is your own version of the stabilization process in therapy. You're finding ways to feel more connected and grounded so you can feel safe.

Now let's take a look at how those old pathways that we formed in childhood influence our beliefs about ourselves and the world today. In the next chapter, we'll dive into attachment theory and explore how profoundly affected we are by our earliest experiences.

PART 2

TWO FOUNDATIONAL THEORIES BEHIND TRAUMA HEALING FOR OUR OPPRESSED BODIES

CHAPTER 3

How Our Relationships Are Shaped by Trauma

Now that we have built a solid understanding of our nervous system on stress and trauma, let's take a look at how our relationships are affected—and even formed—by trauma. For some of us, trauma dates back to our earliest days of childhood. And our earliest relationships with caregivers can be viewed as a sort of blueprint for our connections in adulthood.

UNDERSTANDING OUR EARLIEST ATTACHMENTS

I frequently hear clients of mine say they feel "like a raw nerve." They're not imagining it. Stress and trauma in childhood impact our bodies' ability to create the protective cushioning around our nerves called myelin. If the brain and nervous system form in an unsafe environment, myelination is stunted.[1] Someone with childhood trauma literally has less coating on their nerves, meaning there is less of a buffer between them and the world, and they therefore become more easily overwhelmed.

My client Jo was severely neglected as a child, left to their own devices at far too young an age. They frequently needed care, both physical and emotional, that was not available to them. Like Jo, people whose brains and nervous systems formed in the absence of care can often spend their lives stuck in survival mode. They never got the chance to develop internal emotion regulation because no parent or caregiver ever co-regulated with them. All the networks Jo tuned and pruned in childhood were still their go-to responses.

Before we dive into just how our childhoods affect our developing nervous systems, I think it's important to get up close and personal with the theory considered to be foundational to the psychology of relationships: attachment theory. Let's look at how that blueprint created by our earliest caregivers sheds light on how we see ourselves in the world.

THE GOOD ENOUGH CAREGIVER

In the simplest terms, attachment is the bond between caregiver and child. It is the ability our caregivers had to meet our needs, pay attention to us, attune to us. Attachment develops in the small, everyday moments of connection and care between caregiver and child. Attachment theory is the idea that this early bond sets the tone for a person's relationships with others for their lifetime.

As a mother, I think about this with my child and all of the reciprocal moments we share—how my child makes their needs known and how I instinctively react. My child smiles at me and I smile back. They cry and I comfort them. They try out something new and I encourage them. Now, this is not to say I'm a perfect mother. Far from it. I am simply showing how very simple attachment can be. It is not about being a perfect caregiver. It is simply about being good enough.

In the 1950s British pediatrician, psychologist, and attachment theorist Donald Winnicott came up with the concept of the "good enough" caregiver—the idea that children need a caregiver who is able to meet their emotional and physical needs *well enough* to develop. Children do not need a perfect caregiver; good enough is truly good enough! In fact, perfection would be a bad thing. Perfection would set kids up to expect perfection from everyone: the world, career, future friends, coworkers, lovers. The caregiver who reaches for perfection is creating a blueprint for future relationships that their child will never be able to find again.

But, if it's not perfection, what is *good enough* caregiving exactly?

THE HOLDING ENVIRONMENT

Good enough is simple. The caregiver holds the baby. I don't just mean holds them physically, although that is a huge aspect of it. The caregiver creates what is called the *holding environment*, which the infant needs during the holding phase, the first months after birth. This is the time when babies need their caregivers for everything.

Good enough caregiving means the baby is hardly aware of their environment. If they are cold, they are dressed with more layers, and suddenly they are no longer aware of the temperature because they have been "held." Their needs have been intuited and met.

And as discussed above, it doesn't mean perfection. A good enough caregiving model includes rupture and repair. The caregiver messes up and gets the opportunity to model for their child what accountability can look like and what forgiveness can be.[2]

In his 2002 book, *The Happiest Baby on the Block*, pediatrician and author Harvey Karp popularized the term *the fourth trimester*.[3] His theory is that humans are born too early and that we need another three months of womb-like care. Horses are born able to walk and run within hours of birth. Birds fly from the nest after about ten days. Human babies? We need years of care before we are able to walk or venture out on our own, and in the first three months after birth we need the most care. Winnicott writes that what we need most during this phase is to be physically held. Why? He theorized that this is how babies know they are loved.

When we are babies, we don't know how to self-regulate and need caregivers to regulate us. When we are physically held, we *co-regulate*. Our stressed-out, brand-new nervous systems sync up with our, hopefully, calm and connected caregivers, and we are soothed. Our entire being is dependent on getting that holding environment. Winnicott likens infants in this phase to kernels. It is the good enough caregiver and the holding environment they create that allow us to burst open into individuals. During these early months of life, babies have what is called the Moro reflex. When they are startled, they flail their arms and legs and look shocked or scared. This is because they feel like they are falling. It is the caregiver who creates a physical but also a psychological anchor for babies: "You are not falling, I've got you. I am right here with you."

And what about the caregiver? Why might a caregiver not be "good enough?" Maybe they had childhood trauma of their own and do not know how to be good enough. Maybe they came from a traumatized lineage of caregiving, or lack thereof, and were raised with the idea that babies don't need too much care—that they are resilient and that you spoil them by loving on them too much.

Why might someone believe that? How does this fallacy serve a caregiver? If a baby doesn't need much love, then caregivers do not have to sit with the discomfort of not being able to give them that love and connection. They may not know how to because no one ever showed them. Or maybe they work three part-time jobs to pay the rent and can't slow down to hold their baby because they didn't get even six weeks' parental leave. Maybe they are mentally or physically ill. Maybe they have been incarcerated or separated by a border. Maybe they are struggling with addiction. Maybe they didn't plan on being a parent but couldn't travel somewhere to get a safe abortion. Maybe they didn't plan on being a caregiver at seventy-five but that's what you do when your own child dies and leaves behind a baby.

This is not to say that people who are in these realities are never good enough parents. I will never forget being in a training course where the term *single-parent household* was used to suggest someone had a difficult childhood. A single parent stood up and challenged our bias. Why do we equate this common reality with difficulty? Yes, it is hard to raise a child alone, but that does not mean that child won't get good enough parenting! Touché.

So what if—for whatever reason—a caregiver can't give us what we need, can't be "good enough"? What if they do not have the personal capacity to hold us, to create the holding environment? Winnicott writes, "If [caregiver] care is not good enough then the infant does not really come into existence, since there is no continuity of being; instead the personality becomes built on the basis of reactions to environmental impingement."[4] If we do not receive good enough caregiving, we do not come into existence? Technically, yes, we exist! But the personality becomes a series of reactions, what I will call adaptations to our environment, to our caregiver. "They can't meet my needs? Fine. I won't have any needs. I am cold or hungry or scared and there is no one there to comfort me or give me what I need to not notice my environment? I will stop noticing my body. I will never really live inside of myself."

This is big, huge, intense stuff, I know. However, there is hope within Winnicott's work. (He was a psychoanalyst after all.) His theory for those of us who never got the holding environment, the good enough caregiver? We heal through the consistency and love of the psychoanalyst or therapist: the consistency of sessions and the office, the calm nervous system of the therapist, the endless acceptance and curiosity the client feels from them. Sound familiar? We heal through repeated *mismatched* experiences, and they literally rewire our brain. Every session, every moment of feeling held by the therapist, creates a mismatched experience with those attachment experiences. And as we've already covered and will continue to explore, therapy is not the only way to heal.

My client Jo grew up in the rural Midwest. Their parents worked long hours, had a very "hands off" parenting style, and smoked a lot of weed. When Jo needed comfort as a child, there was no adult around to get it from, and when their parents were around, they were often unavailable or too stoned to pay attention to their child. So Jo found comfort in being alone in the woods behind their home. Mother Nature was the safe holding environment they couldn't get from their parents. Jo would spend hours outside by a wooded creek behind the house. The forest enveloped them in the warm holding environment their parents were too high and checked out to give them. The noise of the creek soothed their nervous system, since they couldn't hear the soothing voice or words of a reassuring parent. In the woods by the creek, Jo could escape into their imagination, or into a fantasy book they would bring to dive into. Here outside, and within their mind, they could go somewhere else, where other lonely kids found magic, friends, and other worlds. Nature, books, and their imagination gave them the childhood their parents neglected to give them. This taught them that being alone is what is safe. "I can get all of my needs met outside in nature and within my own mind."

Experiences of childhood neglect and abuse, and what happens to children who are not provided with "good enough" caregiving is at the heart of the study of relationships, especially attachment theory.

ATTACHMENT AS NOURISHMENT

Also in the 1950s British psychoanalyst John Bowlby was fascinated by how the caregiver-child relationship impacted emotional and psychological health later in life. His experience in institutional settings before, during, and after World War II led him to conduct a study with the World Health Organization (WHO) on the impact of maternal separation on hospitalized and institutionalized children. (It will not surprise you that Ursula Bowlby, John's wife, who was intensely involved in their work, rarely receives credit.)

This was during a time when the dominant belief in Western culture was that too much nurturance and care spoiled a child, that too much physical contact actually harmed babies. Researchers and psychologists at the extreme end of the spectrum speculated that babies only needed food from their mothers and could literally be raised in boxes[5] or on baby farms.[6] Sterile environments were believed to be what was healthiest for a child.

Attachment theorists like Bowlby were revolutionary for his time. He proposed that the attachment relationship is as important to health as getting the right vitamins and minerals. He theorized that children do not bond with their caregivers over feeding, but, rather, through comfort and care. Bowlby speculated that attachment is actually evolutionary, favored by natural selection. Humans survived best when they were extremely dependent on caregivers, on community. This was true for adults as well—those who stayed close to other humans survived, whereas those who left the pack were vulnerable and didn't survive.

American psychologist Harry Harlow was inspired by Bowlby's

work and used Bowlby's maternal deprivation hypothesis as the basis of most of his own work. (Harlow was married to psychologist Margaret Kuenne Harlow, who worked alongside her husband. Yet no one will be shocked that we never learn her name in grad school.) In Harlow's now-infamous 1958 study, baby rhesus monkeys were separated from their mothers. He found that the baby monkeys became very attached to the soft cloths used to cushion the bottom of their wire cages. They would become upset if the cloths were removed. Harlow (and probably Margaret—*say her name!*) noticed this and the wire mother/cloth mother study was born.

They introduced baby monkeys to two surrogate mothers—one, a mother built out of wire that held a bottle of milk, and the other also built of wire, but covered in a soft cloth. The cloth-covered "mother" had nothing to offer foodwise.[7] Each mother had a unique wooden face, which the baby monkeys recognized. They preferred their unique cloth mother over any other. They preferred their cloth mother over the wire mother that fed them. The baby monkeys would get food from the wire mother and spend the rest of the day clutching the cloth mother, especially going to her for comfort when they were scared.

It is absolutely devastating to look at photos of these infants, literally clinging to their soft cloth pad in their cage or holding on tight to a bizarre handmade wire and cloth and wood structure for comfort. It is heartbreaking because it is certainly animal abuse, but also because these monkeys look so similar to human babies. This is how desperate we are for comfort and contact, how vital those are to a child.

An Acknowledgment of a Violent History

We cannot talk about attachment theory without also acknowledging the brutal history of white Western colonization that removed Indigenous children from their families and forced them into residential boarding schools in the US. And think of children being taken from their parents during enslavement and *sold* as chattel. This is baked into the horrific history of America, perpetrated by the same white, Western culture that promoted the practice of physically and emotionally neglecting children as the best way to parent. And it's happening now to children as they are separated from caregivers at borders.

Popular parenting trends today are really just the attachment-based parenting most of the world has always implemented with their children. Co-sleeping, babywearing, gentle parenting, Mommunes (single moms living and raising their kids together), baby-led weaning, and including your children in daily activities like cooking, gardening, and so on are all basic parenting practices that came long before some men in white coats "created" parenting theories.[8]

ATTACHMENT STYLES

Now we're getting to the nitty-gritty—the origins of the theory of attachment styles—so that you can better understand your own attachment style, how it was formed, and how it plays out for you in adult relationships. You've heard people refer to themselves as having an "anxious" attachment style or as being "anxious-avoidant." Well, we can thank American Canadian developmental psychologist

Mary Ainsworth for these designations. She gained recognition for her famous 1970 Strange Situation[9] study with Silvia Bell, where they set up a playroom with a two-way mirror to observe a parent and a child interact. In a series of "strange situations," the parent and child enter a room and are joined by a stranger. At one point the parent leaves and then returns. The stranger does the same. This scenario was believed to illustrate the children's attachment styles. The one-to-two-year-old children were scored on their separation anxiety, their ability to freely explore the playroom, how they reacted to the stranger, and, most of all, how they felt when the parent returned from their absence. Observations were put into the following categories: how physically close they kept themselves to the parent and how they interacted with them, the amount of time they remained close to the parent, whether they avoided closeness or interacting, whether they actively resisted closeness or interaction, and whether they went searching for the parent.

All participants were white middle-class Americans. There is no note in the study of the sexuality, ability, or mental health of the caregivers in the study, and they were also all mothers. The strange situation did not include fathers or other types of caregivers such as aunts/uncles, godparents, or grandparents. Because all of the participants were American, attachment styles were really created around the impact of white, middle-class, heteronormative American parenting, and American parenting ideals. For example, in cultures that instill more independence and freedom into their child-rearing, caregivers may not get the same enthusiastic reunion as with an American child, but that doesn't mean that the child feels less "held" or loved.

In spite of the limitations of the study, the results remain intriguing. Ainsworth came up with the following attachment styles to describe the babies in her study: resistant, avoidant, and secure.[10] *Re-*

sistant is what we now refer to as *anxious*. She categorized the behavior in the following ways:

- *Anxious* (formerly *resistant*): These children were extremely distressed when the parent left but were unable to be comforted when the parent returned.
- *Avoidant*: These children might be distressed when the caregiver left but avoided or ignored their caregivers upon their return.
- *Secure*: These children had a healthy level of distress when the caregiver left the room, showing they were bonded, and they were comforted when the caregiver returned.

A fourth category was added by psychologists Mary Main and Judith Solomon. Using the results of the Strange Situation study, they found that some children were "unclassifiable"[11] and did not fit any of the three main attachment styles. They referred to this group as having *disorganized attachment*, what we now refer to as

- *Anxious-avoidant*: These children seemed to both want and avoid their caregiver but then reacted in fear when the caregiver responded to them.

Let's take a closer look at each attachment style.

Anxious Attachment

Children with anxious attachment miss their caregivers when they are at work, but when they come home stressed and distracted, children aren't able to co-regulate and attune their nervous systems to a caregiver's calm nervous system. The child is miserable when their caregiver is gone, and still miserable when they come home. Or they may be soothed momentarily by the caregiver, but the comfort is fleeting.

Adults who have a more anxious attachment style may not have gotten the co-regulation they needed in their earliest relationships. There was no calm nervous system to attune to and show their nervous system how to relax. Or their caregivers were overly attentive and hovering, meaning the child was forced to be overreliant on someone else for soothing and never taught self-soothing or what is called autoregulation. Anxious attachment commonly occurs in children who are focused on making sure their caregivers are "okay," doing this through parentified caretaking, codependency, people pleasing, and pushing down their own emotions and needs. This leaves kids and, later, adults anxious as they have had nowhere to go with their own emotions, as well as anxious about their relationships because they are so used to focusing on others and making sure everything is okay for everyone else.

The term *anxious attachment* has always made me imagine myself pacing my apartment waiting for my ex-girlfriend to come home from drinking all night at the bar and berate me. I was anxious waiting for her to come back, hoping to be soothed by her arrival ("When she's home, I can go to bed, we can connect, I can feel more regulated"), only to be in more distress when she finally arrived. But I held on to the hope, the desire, that my reunion with her would soothe me. She was unable to do this, as many caregivers are not able to do.

If you were anxiously attached in childhood, you will probably show up in your adult relationships seeking that co-regulation you didn't get or didn't get enough of. This can look like:[12]

- Difficulty emotionally regulating, struggling to get back into your window of tolerance without another person.

- Having a hard time knowing your needs and naming them to others.
- Feeling like you can't take up space with feelings.
- Feedback that your needs are too much or too overwhelming for others.
- People pleasing to keep others close or happy with you, even if it leads to self-abandonment.
- Feeling like you need to be in more constant communication with people in your life because it is overwhelming to be alone.
- Excessive relational checking, seeking reassurance from friends and lovers: "Are we good?"

But let's also talk about the bright side of being an anxiously attached adult. These people really value close and intimate relationships. Anxiously attached folks are very attuned to others' needs. They have an easy time being caretakers for others, and the people in their life really value that. Anxiously attached people are extremely loving, effusive, and available for those they care about. If this is you, it's all about balancing to make sure you're not giving too much and leaving your cup empty.

Avoidant Attachment

Avoidant attachment can occur for a number of reasons: A caregiver can be overbearing or overinvolved in a child's life, and that kid can grow up seeking space from others as a way to get freedom. The avoidant attachment here is an act of self-preservation—space means I can be my own person, and means I won't get emotionally overwhelmed by another. Avoidant attachment can occur for the opposite reason too: when caregivers are neglectful and/or abusive. *Avoidant* here doesn't mean children don't care about their caregiver or don't need them. In fact, they are distressed and express it through avoidance. "It feels better to tell myself I don't need you than to allow myself to need you." "Distance feels safer, even though I am still distressed by your absence." Avoidant children still need parents. But they have adapted to become avoidant toward them to survive, like my client Jo.

As a child, Jo was lonely and afraid most days, with no safe adult or even another human being to go to with these feelings. Ideally, childhood is the time to learn how to manage these big feelings, which Jo never learned. They also never got the chance to learn that closeness can be safe and regulating, so now, when someone pursues them as a friend or as a romantic partner, they immediately feel like the person is trying to take over their life. They get "the ick." You would think that all Jo would want is someone to finally be close to, but in fact that experience is too much and threatens what they have built to experience safety: time alone in nature. This is what is predictable and known. Intimacy is overwhelming because it is a foreign concept.

If you had a more avoidant attachment style as a child, you might experience:

- Difficulty regulating with other people and a general preference for being alone.
- Stress or not feeling at ease with other people, even those who are close to you.
- Ease connecting with nature, animals, and social activities with some distance involved.
- A belief that there is a person out there who is perfect for you, which creates challenges in getting close to others because you aren't sure if there might be someone better for you out there.
- Challenges committing in relationships: romantic, friendship, and work related.

But being avoidant isn't all negative, and this adaptive response can actually show up in really beautiful ways as an adult. If you are more avoidant, you might also feel more at ease with change, moving apartments or cities, changing careers. People might come to you for more honesty since you are not fixated on people pleasing and saying the perfect thing. If you are avoidant, you might be very picky about who you do allow to get close to you, which can lead to really deep and fulfilling relationships with just a few people.

Secure Attachment

Securely attached children have a bond with the caregiver that allows them to feel close with them but not dependent upon them to the point of extreme separation anxiety. The securely attached babies in the Ainsworth study used the caregiver as their safe base to explore the playroom and were soothed by the return of the caregiver, in contrast to anxiously attached babies who weren't soothed by the reunion and avoidant babies who didn't react at all. Caregivers foster a secure attachment by staying attuned to their child. They sense their needs, emotional needs in particular, and try to meet them. A caregiver picks up on these needs without verbal communication.

If you were securely attached as a child, you might:

- Desire connection and have the ability to experience it with others.
- Know your needs and feel comfortable in naming them to others.
- Believe that the world and other people are generally good most of the time.
- Be able to co-regulate with other people and feel at ease with those who you are close to.

- Feel in touch with your body and be able to meet its needs, and feel as though you live inside yourself, not on the outside.
- Possess emotion regulation skills that work, and be able to come back into your window of tolerance with some ease.

Being securely attached has a lot of obvious benefits in adulthood: knowing one's self and needs, being connected to one's body, wanting to be close to others but not desperately needing it, having a solid sense of self. A secure attachment literally creates a safety buffer (that nerve covering called myelin) between you and the world. The nervous system is more regulated. The brain functions more smoothly. It's not that someone who had a secure attachment with a caregiver as a child or has one in a current relationship is guaranteed an easy life, but parts of their life are certainly easier than for someone without a secure attachment. A secure attachment in childhood is a privilege. And someone can have the privilege of a secure attachment but not have other privileges, so life can still be stressful, hard, and even traumatic. But how that secure person copes or is affected by that stress or trauma is different from someone without that foundation.

I believe we all contain a secure part of ourselves, even if we didn't get a secure attachment from a caregiver. This is called our Self-energy, which we will learn about in the next chapter. I believe we can create secure attachments to parts of ourselves, even if that isn't what we were able to form in childhood.

Anxious-Avoidant Attachment, aka Disorganized Attachment

The children in the Strange Situation study who exhibited disorganized attachment were determined by social services to have experienced[13] abuse or neglect at higher rates than children who fit into the other categories. The anxious-avoidant children in Main and Solomon's study reacted to the return of their caregivers with fear and self-protection, like holding hands up in front of their faces. Studies have shown that children with the disorganized attachment style have higher cortisol levels than the kids who fit the traditional three categories.[14]

Disorganized attachment is described as showing conflicting behavior: The child avoids the parent but then wants them; the child tries to engage with the parent but then screams when the parent comes to be with them. Essentially, "I want to be close, but I don't know how. I want you to get away from me, but I miss you when you go."[15] This attachment style is all tangled up with the person's survival instincts. Studies show that disorganized attachment is correlated with extreme nervous system dysregulation and dissociation.[16]

When children are abused or neglected by caregivers, their big, overwhelming feelings have no safe way to be expressed. Some children don't express this dysregulation outwardly and it gets internalized as extreme anxiety. Disorganized attachment shows up as our old friend complex PTSD (cPTSD).

My client Vee feels this attachment style with their wife, when they are experiencing a trigger. Their wife will try to comfort them, and Vee will try to accept that care, but it doesn't help because they are too far into their trauma-triggered state. Instead, they want lots of space away from their wife because her love can feel triggering too. When Vee is deep in their childhood trauma, that love can feel dangerous, like they will somehow get hurt if they accept it, or if they let themselves enjoy the safety and comfort, because of the huge risk that they could lose it.

If you had a disorganized attachment in childhood, in adulthood you might:

- Feel disconnected from your body, dissociated.
- Fear getting close to others.
- Desire to be close to others and then want them to go away when they do finally get close.
- Believe you are unworthy, not good enough, bad.
- Be unable to feel safe, even when safety is available.
- Struggle to feel connected to a core Self.
- Feel not real, not human.

The upside of being disorganized in attachment? It often leads people to immense personal growth, healing, and searching for more in life. My clients are in so much pain and distress as a result of their childhoods and the impact of them on their adulthoods. These are people who are often asking big existential questions in therapy like, "My parents never should have had children. Why am I here?" or "How did I survive my childhood? I must have a bigger purpose." By engaging with these questions, these clients tend to find a spiritual meaning in their very existence. Against all odds, they are alive and safe today, so there must be a plan that the universe had for them. This isn't to say that the abuse was "worth it" or that it should have happened. But they are here, they did survive, so what do they want from their life? For someone who is a survivor, this question means something even deeper.

When a child grows up with no model for how to self-regulate or be close to others, their brain tunes and prunes according to a chaotic and abusive environment. Think of what neural networks get established here. What pathways die off? Remember, however, that you can create new pathways through mismatches—the way Vee has done through therapy, a safe relationship, and in other ways we'll explore.

ATTACHMENT STYLES—IT'S NOT THAT SIMPLE

Just as with the question of nature versus nurture, attachment is much more complicated than the definitions imply. Factors include our caregivers' own childhoods and life circumstances, neurodiversity, our own ever-evolving lives. The truth is that attachment is not a fixed set of rules. Depending on the relationship itself, the dynamic with the other person, and where we are in our healing journey, we may have different attachment styles with different people. We may show up anxious in one relationship, avoidant in the next, and then meet someone who is a better fit and after having done a lot of hard work on ourselves be able to be secure.

Our attachment experience with a caregiver can be due to the caregiver's own attachment style and the impact of their childhood. Many of us grew up with caregivers who needed us to become the parents, to be the one checking the vibe and becoming what was needed. "Mom is sad? I will become the happy kid and cheer her up!" "Dad is angry? I will become invisible so as to not get in his way, or I will try and make everything perfect so he doesn't explode." "Grandma, who is raising me, is sick? I will become a caregiver."

Another factor for our own style is the caregiver's daily lived experience of stress. There's a reason the first question you are often asked as a new parent is "Are they eating well? Sleeping through the night yet?" This is code for "Oh my god, are you okay?" As a new mother, I got a full taste of this. When my baby was eating well, sleeping well, enjoying coming along for long hikes and road trips, I felt like I had more capacity to connect and bond with them. When my child hit the four-month sleep regression, I recognized that as a sleep-deprived parent, I didn't have the same emotional and physical capacity. I definitely wasn't my best self during that time.

Caregivers alone aren't the only reason our attachment styles develop. Some babies are just born more or less sensitive. I hear from parents all the time that one of their kids was born with a more reactive nervous system than their other child. Some babies adapt to their caregivers right away, sensing that the caregiver needs a child with fewer needs. Other babies just need less soothing or are more flexible.

Attachment affects much more than our ability to connect with others. Our experiences in our early years impact how we see ourselves in the world. My client Jo likes to talk about attachment as the foundation of life, and if you experience misattunement, abuse, or neglect, your brain, body, and sense of self never benefit from that strong foundation. For someone who never developed a secure attachment, never got that co-regulation and the neural cushioning that secure attachment provides, when life gets hard, it tends to stay hard. If we didn't get that buffer from the world as kids, it's very hard—but not impossible—to get that buffer later.

This chapter might feel heavy, but it is important to really sit with the reality of the impact of these early years on us—and know that just like it is with our neural pathways, healing is possible. We can give ourselves attachment experiences we never got. We can literally learn how to *reparent* ourselves.

CREATING AN ATTACHMENT MISMATCH

How do attachment styles show up in our adult lives in romantic partnerships and friendships? We often tend to be attracted to people with an attachment style similar to that of our caregivers. These people feel like home, whether we recognize that or not. Our brain, nervous system, and attachment style recognize that familiarity and drive us toward it. If we had absent or cruel caregivers, are we doomed to the same kind of relationship in adulthood? No. But it will take a lot of extra work not to partner with people who remind us, often without us even realizing it, of our caregivers.

Imago is an attachment-based couples' therapy technique that suggests we have a composite image of every person who cared for us when we were young, and we are drawn to those who remind us of that composite.[17] This helps us understand how we end up in the same kind of relationships over and over, often choosing people who mimic those who wounded us in childhood. We search for a corrective experience, going back to the same conditions hoping for a new outcome.

This is how so many members of my community and my clients end up in relationships with people who can't see or validate them, just like their family of origin couldn't. Most of the time we can't explain why we feel drawn to people. Someone can feel familiar or intoxicating even if we can't draw a direct connection to one of our caregivers, or that composite image, the imago. Someone may feel "like home" because of implicit memories, those memories that live inside our bodies as feelings.

Attachment shows up in adulthood in how we feel about ourselves and the world. I see this in beliefs about our self-worth. Winnicott said babies know they are loved by being held. For those of us who didn't get that holding environment, how do we know we are loveable? If we had no secure base to come back to, how can we trust other people to be safe, or that the world is a safe place for us to explore? If our needs were shamed or ignored, how can we believe it's okay to have needs, to take up space? How do we show up in our authenticity if we experienced rejection from those who were supposed to help us explore who we are?

If we did not get these attachment experiences as children, we have to get them in adulthood, through a mismatch—that experience that defies our earlier experiences and establishes new possibilities.

It's hard to experience a mismatch if we keep dating people who remind us of home. It's hard to experience a mismatch if the world reinforces our sense of unworthiness, which it especially does for queer and trans people, and for anyone at the margins.

If our caregivers couldn't hold us, we can find the holding experience in therapy, in community, in nature, and, yes, even in ourselves. It is through these forms of being held that we can create mismatches and tune those new, nourishing pathways of secure attachment.

Community as a Holding Environment

The theory that attachment is evolutionary underpins a core tenet of trauma healing from oppression: *community*. Community is vital for happiness, connection, and healing. We physically need other people to survive. If we do not stay close to the pack, we die. Obviously, this is true when we are vulnerable babies and children, but what about later in life? We don't just suddenly stop needing other people just because we can meet our own basic needs. All those years ago, it was the queer community that saved me. I needed other queers, as Winnicott says, "to come into existence, to feel real." It was through my romantic, sexual, and chosen family relationships that I found my true sense of self as a lesbian woman. I am not just talking about becoming real because I figured out my sexuality. I became real because the thing about me that had never quite fit anywhere—my queerness, my difference, my core Self—was finally seen and celebrated. First we come out, whatever that looks like for us, and then we become real.

People can create new attachment experiences for one another when we create community. Many of us might not have gotten the care and acceptance we needed from our family of origin, so we have become experts in getting this need met from our community, our chosen family. It is never too late to attach. It is never too late to become real.

For many queer and trans people I know, their caregiver attachments were disrupted somewhere along the way due to rejection of their differentness, a differentness often unconsciously detected by their caregiver. But when we are rejected by our families of origin, we can create new attachments. I became real on sweaty dance floors at gay bars, in secret sex dungeons, under a tattoo gun, on the streets during Dyke March and protests, and mostly naked by the ocean with hundreds of other queer and trans folks at the Jacob Riis beach in Queens, New York. When we are turned away by those who raised us, community becomes our good enough caregiver. It's rarely perfect, but it is often good enough.

For so many of us, our healing extends past or has only existed outside of the therapy room, in the streets, in the arms of our lovers, through radical art, or in prayer spaces, nature, and more. While many of us who have had these experiences know well that this is part of our journey, our recovery, I have rarely seen this confirmed or validated as healing too.

Nature as a Holding Environment

As a child, my client Jo did not get the holding environment they needed. In fact, they had to cut themselves off from the part of them that needed caregivers. They learned that they felt more comforted and held in the woods behind their home than inside it. Fast-forward to the present day. Jo struggles to let people be close to them. In their spare time, they hike the Pacific Crest Trail and the Appalachian Trail for days on end, completely on their own. They truly feel like they do not need other humans and are happiest alone in the woods. Usually they avoid relationships, but when they allow someone to get close, they are very quick to walk away and experience no real distress when the relationship ends, just extreme relief.

This is something Jo is working on. But when they need to feel at home in their body, to feel real, they know that they can always find it in nature, in the woods, in a hammock between trees, hearing the *thonk thonk* of their hiking boots on the trail.

Finding the Holding Environment Within

My client Vee grew up in a chaotic, unpredictable, and cold environment. No one said "I love you," and no one offered comfort or care when things were scary or hard. Vee didn't have a caregiver with a regulated nervous system to help them co-regulate. They constantly felt like they were doing something wrong, or even that there was something inherently wrong with them. As a child, Vee could not allow themselves to relax and drop their guard—they didn't feel comfortable creating art or even napping.

Our work together focused on Vee building a safe, secure attachment with themselves. Vee spent hours in our sessions imagining sitting with their child self, getting to know this part of them, hearing what childhood was like, and imagining transporting their child self out of their abusive and chaotic home into their Safe Place: an imagined cabin in the woods. Here, Vee and their child self enjoyed activities they had never felt "safe enough" doing growing up: engaging in creative projects, exploring, resting. Vee gave their child self what therapist Janina Fisher calls "missing experiences," the holding environment they didn't get in childhood that would have fostered a secure attachment. Vee could build one in the here and now with their inner child. "Growing up, I felt like an animal. Focused on survival, not able to be in touch with my humanity. Now, for the first time in my life, I feel human. I feel emotions. I feel love toward people in my life." This is the healing a secure attachment can offer those of us who didn't get one as children. We can find secure attachment with a partner, of course, but we can also find it in our community, in nature, or, as Vee did, within ourselves.

YOUR TURN

Let's pause and take a deep breath together. Think of someone or something—a beloved person, place, animal, or object—that holds you, that makes you feel that your needs are met. What happens in your body when you think of them/it? How has this good enough person, place, or thing given you love, made you feel secure enough? Maybe it's your Safe Place. Maybe you can choose someone/something new and add one more rung onto your ladder of getting to "safe enough." Each time you think of your attachment with this person, place, or thing, you will create a mismatch to anytime you did not feel held.

I imagine myself floating on my back in the river of my childhood that is my own Safe Place. When I was living in New York City away from the river for a decade, I used the Atlantic Ocean as my Safe Place, my water mother. For me, there is nothing as soothing as being rocked by the waves or feeling the river pull around my body in a gentle flow.

Where are you? Or who are you with? Stay with them a little longer, taking one more deep breath. When you feel grounded again, back inside yourself, read on.

BRINGING IT ALL TOGETHER

We have dug deep into attachment theory and its origins. Just like our class, race, gender, ability, and more, our attachment experiences shape our access to privilege and safety in the world. If we got a secure base, life can be more gentle on us. If we did not get what we needed as children, if we were actively harmed and abused during these deeply impactful years of our lives, everything is and feels harder. Our attachment style doesn't just impact who we date in our teenage and adult years, as it is popularly used to describe. It determines how we move through the world, how we feel about ourselves, what feels possible for us. It determines how well we listen to our bodies, if we even live inside our own bodies. Our attachment experience creates narratives about worthiness, safety, and our needs as human beings.

There *is* hope in all of this. Just like our nervous system can learn to feel safe, just like our brain can rewire toward adaptive networks, our attachment system can rewire itself too. In chapter 6, we'll explore healing attachment wounds and childhood trauma. But before we get there, we have one more foundational theory to explore. In the next chapter, we will dig into *parts work*, a way of healing that creates a secure attachment with all parts of yourself, giving your younger parts the attuned and loving attachment experience very few of us actually got.

CHAPTER 4

How Our Sense of Self Is Shaped by Trauma

My client Carlos came to our work together wanting to heal from complex PTSD. As a child, Carlos had experienced a traumatic separation from his parents and subsequent immigration to the US, but he had never processed it in therapy. He had spent his earlier therapy sessions in stabilization: learning about trauma and how to understand and identify his triggers, and building stabilization tools for the here and now like Safe Place, Container, and learning how to return to his window of tolerance. This all made it possible for him to manage his depression and anxiety so that he could hold down a job and care for himself on a basic level. Carlos and I began our processing work together by getting curious about how his inner system of "parts" functioned. Only then could Carlos learn how to find compassion, community, and freedom within.

Most of my trans clients and loved ones knew they were trans from the time they were two to four years old. I myself knew I was queer at ten. Most queer and trans folks were forced to exile those core parts of themselves at a young age in order to fit in, stay safe, and get love. For my clients who have experienced sexual trauma, they have learned to distance themselves from the part that experienced that trauma in order to function in everyday life and be intimate with partners.

We still live in a society where so many are forced to stay in the closet, feel daily shame about their sexual desires and their bodies, or mask cultural, neurodiverse (including mental health issues), or unwell parts of themselves in order to gain acceptance. We have learned that we cannot show up 100 percent authentically, in all our parts, in all our pain. We rely on numbing behaviors, including substance abuse, like Sam did. Or we dissociate like Jessy, feeling far away from ourselves. Addictive behavior and dissociation are just two ways we protect our traumatized parts that we've cut ourselves off from in order to survive in a homophobic, transphobic, racist, and patriarchal world.

Parts work is the process of getting to know all those inner parts of ourselves, to understand how some parts protect the more vulnerable parts, and to invite those long-hidden parts to come forward, unburden themselves, and ultimately come together so we can feel whole again—or possibly for the first time.

Parts work is essential to trauma healing for our oppressed bodies. More than anyone else, those of us living at the margins are asked to fragment ourselves to survive in this world and to become what others want or need us to be instead of our true, authentic selves. Parts work is radically transformative for those of us who learn these harmful lessons about fragmenting ourselves for survival—not just in our family of origins but in the world at large—because it allows us to come back to ourselves, to accept and embrace the parts of us that have been exiled. Parts work weaves our attachment system back together, this time with ourselves.

Before we look at how this process helped Carlos heal, let's take a look at the history of the theory itself so you can understand how it can work for you.

THE HISTORY OF PARTS THEORY

The concept of the self as made up of many parts has been a core belief of spiritual traditions across the world since time immemorial. In ancient Egypt, the soul was believed to be made up of multiple parts: the body (khat), the consciousness (ba), the personality (ren), the essence of self (ka), the shadow self (khaibit), the heart (ab), the immortal self (akh), the spiritual body (sahu), and the life force (sekhem).[1] In the Bible, humans have three parts: the spirit, the soul, and the body. In the Quran, there are three stages of the self: the lower self (al nafs al ammara bil su), the self-blaming self (al nafs al lawwama), and the reassured self (al nafs al mutmaina). In the Zohar, an ancient text of Jewish mysticism, the soul has five parts: the physical body (nefesh), the emotions (ruach), the intellect (neshama), the knowledge of the divine (chaya), and the pure essence of soul (yechida).[2]

In Western psychotherapy, the three-parts theory emerged with Sigmund Freud in 1923.[3] He theorized that humans contain the id, which is in search of pleasure and avoids pain at all costs, also known as our "animal instinct."[4] Then there's Freud's superego, which is responsible for morality, and between the id and the superego sits the ego, which modulates between the two—kind of an angel/devil on your shoulder thing.

In 1921 psychologist and colleague of Freud's Carl Jung presented his theory: that the psyche is made up of archetypes we inherit from the collective unconscious.[5] One of these is the self: the central part that holds our core essence. Here, our consciousness and unconsciousness merge. Another archetype is the child, from which "inner child work" in Western psychotherapy was born. This remains a popular concept in therapy today, and many therapists and analysts believe that the purpose of psychotherapy is to heal our wounded inner child.[6]

In the early 1970s Heinz Kohut[7] presented self psychology, which presents the self, much like Jung, the core part of which the other parts are fragments. Healing means bringing these fragments back together and creating a more cohesive whole.

The importance of the historical context of these theories can't be underestimated: Freud and Jung were working out their theories through World War I and in the period running up to World War II, and Kohut during the Vietnam War. Psychotherapists were trying to understand how and why humans are capable of such inhumanity, and how people mentally survived these extreme circumstances.

In the 1970s we also saw the emergence of Adult Children of Alcoholics and Dysfunctional Families (ACA), a twelve-step program for those who grew up in a chaotic environment and/or were raised by caregivers who used substances. ACA is focused on healing the inner child and helping the "adult child" learn coping and communication skills they never got from their neglectful caregivers.

In the early 2000s the Theory of Structural Dissociation was developed based on the centuries-old work of the French physician, philosopher, and psychotherapist Pierre Janet. Janet theorized in the late 1800s that when a person survives extreme abuse and/or trauma over many years, especially in childhood, the personality is forced to separate into parts that may even be unknown to each other.

Carlos felt he could relate to this. As a young boy, his parents had left him with family members in Brazil, going to the US to set up a life for the three of them there. He was too young at the time to understand what was happening and was inconsolable for months until he eventually shut down his emotions completely. Even though his parents had left to try to create a "better life" for him, he felt—and in some ways was—abandoned. During the years his parents were in the US, Carlos was sexually abused by a family member and believed he had nowhere to go to talk about or get away from this trauma. Once his parents sent for him, he was suddenly thrust into a culture, language, and place he knew nothing about. His parents were strangers to him, and he felt shame and guilt about it. He struggled to assimilate and refused to speak English. Eventually, after getting in trouble at school enough times, he gave up and gave in, becoming the perfect citizen and son. As a teen Carlos was a straight-A student, and as an adult he is a perfectionist at work and, by all appearances, a high-functioning person.

But he realized that those frightened childhood parts of himself had been buried in order to survive. And he had lost touch with them. Through understanding the Theory of Structural Dissociation, Carlos began to see how it might be possible to reconnect with those hidden parts of himself, process his early trauma, and begin to heal.

THE THEORY OF STRUCTURAL DISSOCIATION: THE FOUNDATION OF PARTS WORK

The Theory of Structural Dissociation holds that people experiencing trauma have two types of parts: *apparently normal parts* (ANPs) that show up and go to school, go to work, and get things done around the house even though there is abuse and trauma unfolding. These parts remain even after the trauma has ended, keeping a highly traumatized person like Carlos high functioning, or as functioning as possible. The other type of parts are *emotional parts* (EPs). These parts hold the emotions and memories from traumatic experiences, as well as the survival responses to keep the person alive.[8] For Carlos, these

EPs stem from childhood as well as from the ongoing oppression-based trauma he experiences as a gay immigrant of color.

There are three levels of structural dissociation: primary, secondary, and tertiary.

In *primary structural dissociation*, the person has experienced a major trauma and has PTSD, but the trauma probably occurred later in life when that person already had a solid foundation of self. There is one ANP that runs the show of functioning on a day-to-day basis, and one EP that holds the memories and emotions from the big trauma they experienced. In theory, someone with PTSD has a core Self that they were able to develop safely in childhood, which would assist them through their healing journey of recovering from PTSD. When the EP overwhelms the system, the person experiences triggers, flashbacks, and all of those PTSD symptoms we covered in chapter 1.

Secondary structural dissociation describes those of us who have dealt with chronic, ongoing trauma, usually beginning in childhood. There is one ANP, the part that showed up at school and got good grades, despite all that was happening at home. Then, there are many EPs that hold memories and emotions from ongoing, sustained trauma. Most people with secondary structural dissociation have a disorganized attachment style. Remember how those kids showed conflicting and confusing attachment responses? This is because a different part of them needed to show up depending on which survival response would get them through the moment or the day. For example, when the abusive parent walks in the door, EPs assess the situation to see how they need to show up to survive. Mom is mad? Better flee to the woods out back so as to not get in her warpath. Mom is sad? Better become the soothing parent she needs me to be.

Tertiary structural dissociation occurs when there are not only many EPs but also several ANPs. This is called *dissociative identity disorder*

(DID).[9] In the past, it has been terribly misunderstood as "multiple personality disorder."[10] DID is more common than people think, because it doesn't typically present as a person who has different names for each self or packs ten lunches to see which self decides to show up at mealtime. It most often presents when a person has had an extremely violent childhood and adult life, ones more severe than the life experiences of someone with secondary structural dissociation. According to the Theory of Structural Dissociation, people with tertiary structural dissociation have multiple ANPs in addition to multiple EPs, because life has been that unsafe and traumatizing that even the ANP is fragmented.

Dissociation as a Defense Mechanism

As you learned in chapter 1, during a trauma, dissociating is our body's final line of defense, when our nervous system has determined it is safest to shut off and play dead in order to survive. In a study of survivors, researchers found that during sexual abuse, the body may go into what is called tonic immobility, a set of physiological responses to a life-threatening situation that allows our bodies to shut down while still being alive. These responses include things like "temporary muscular paralysis (resulting in an inability to fight off an attacker or call out for help), lowered body temperature, uncontrollable tremors, and analgesia."[11] After the sexual abuse or rape, the survivor often has a difficult time *not* using dissociation during stress or a trigger. This is especially true if that person was abused more than once, and even more so if it occurred over a period of years.

Dissociation is not just linked with sexual abuse or other traumatic events in childhood but also present in people who experienced absent or neglectful caregivers. A prolonged lack of feeling seen, loved, and cared for has a lasting effect. Kids get through neglect by checking out, and for some of us, it is really hard to check back in to our lives. Most people with dissociative disorders began to dissociate in childhood, regardless of how violent or stereotypically "bad" they consider their childhoods to have been. In fact, research shows that prolonged verbal abuse has similar effects on the developing brain as sexual abuse.[12] This isn't to compare or rank childhood trauma but rather to show how one doesn't need to be physically abused in childhood to have complex trauma symptoms.

On the more severe end of the spectrum, some people with dissociation experience depersonalization or derealization. With depersonalization, people feel removed from themselves, like they are watching their lives happen on TV or in a book they are reading. Derealization is where they feel like the world around them or they themselves are unreal, like they are part of or living in a video game or a dream. They may even feel like a robot.

Dissociation on a Spectrum

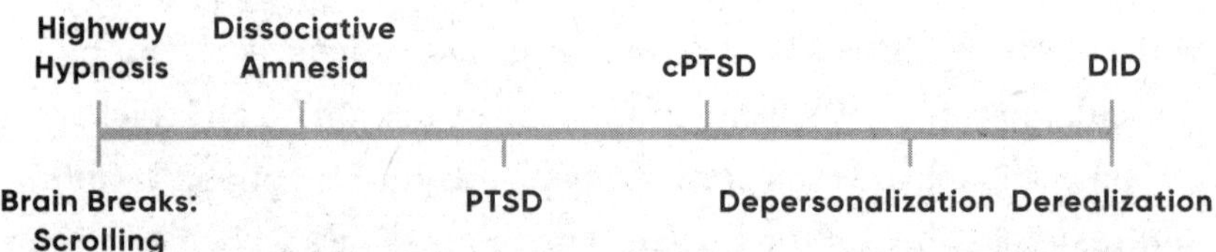

The term *dissociation* may make us think of an extreme form of out-of-body experience, or a person with DID who suffered extreme childhood trauma, but the truth is that we all dissociate sometimes to varying degrees. Dissociation exists on a spectrum.

We're on the mild end of the spectrum when we zone out in the middle of a conversation, while we scroll mindlessly on our phones only to be surprised that twenty minutes have gone by, or when we drive somewhere and then don't remember parts of the trip. We give our brain little breaks from all it does for us throughout the day.

DID is on the extreme end of the spectrum.

Most of us who have experienced significant trauma and stress fall somewhere in the middle. We find ourselves using dissociation all the time, which is when it becomes a survival coping strategy. As we'll learn in the next section, dissociation can be one of our internal parts that protects us.

INTERNAL FAMILY SYSTEMS (IFS): PARTS WORK IN AND OUT OF THE THERAPY ROOM

Today, the most popular parts-work modality in psychotherapy offices is known as Internal Family Systems (IFS), developed in the 1980s by therapist Richard Schwartz. Because it is extremely accessible and relatable, people can use it on their own to work on their trauma healing. While parts work draws from the European theories of Janet, Freud, and Jung, it also has similarities with Indigenous belief systems. And in fact Schwartz has received criticism that IFS is a watered-down and repackaged version of different Indigenous healing traditions. Many Indigenous spiritual leaders and Indigenous IFS therapists have taken the modality and returned it to its rightful container.

When Schwartz began developing IFS, most of his clients were in recovery for eating disorders. He found that working with different parts of the Self was more effective than assuming the client had what he calls a mono-mind. He applied systems theory to psychotherapy, using the idea that any whole is made up of many parts—the way a government, a family, and a culture are. In a family system, the members of the family together make up the whole. Each member of the family helps to create the family dynamic. In family systems therapy, each person within the family is seen to hold a role. Sometimes those roles are appropriate, like when the caregiver is in a caregiving role. Other times, it's an inappropriate role, like when a child is forced into a caregiving role. Family systems therapy helps individuals look at their role in the family and, if it isn't functioning or appropriate, learn how to switch roles and have balance created or restored within the family unit.

Schwartz took the family systems concept to a new level. He saw his clients' inner parts as having roles within what he calls an internal family system. These inner parts took on certain roles—he calls them burdens—due to early childhood experiences and traumatic events. His goal for clients is to help them build an awareness of their inner parts, create a loving relationship toward those parts, and hear them out so they can unburden themselves of harmful roles that are no longer serving them.

Another way to think about parts that tends to land right away with any client I work with is to conceptualize our parts as an inner family. Within this family, there is an inner child, an inner teen, an inner critical parent, and an inner loving parent. This is just another reworking of the same theory that underlies most parts work.

IFS is different from other types of therapies in important ways. Modalities such as cognitive behavioral therapy (CBT) invite clients to change their thinking to change how they feel. But there is no way to think your way out of trauma or daily oppression. IFS doesn't ask us to diminish the impact of traumatic experiences, rejecting entire parts of ourselves all over again by telling ourselves a new way of thinking. Instead it works on helping our parts feel "safe enough" to feel and think differently.

Let's take a look at IFS to see how it helped Carlos and how it can help you too.

PARTS 101: PROTECTORS, EXILES, AND SELF

IFS theorizes we have three kinds of parts: protective parts of our system that take on burdens to keep us safe, younger exiled parts that hold our big feelings and memories, and the Self—who we truly are at our core—in the center.

Let's take a deep dive into each of these parts.

Meet Your Protectors: Managers and Firefighters

We have two kinds of protective parts: managers and firefighters. Managers quite literally *manage* our lives—they manage other people, show up at work, get shit done. These parts often block us from feeling. They are high functioning, or seem to be. They keep us going, but at a cost of disconnection with our core Self. Examples of manager parts include perfectionist parts, codependent parts, and overworking parts. Most of us have an inner critic part, which is a manager of sorts. This inner critic tends to be the internalization of our critical caregivers and/or society.

I have quite a few manager parts myself. There's the "scheduler," who manages my use of time and often doesn't make space for rest or unstructured creativity. Sometimes I realize she has taken over my internal system and I've been looking at my calendar for an hour, just blocking off time, moving things around, trying to make the most "optimal" use of my time. My inner critic has internalized the criticism I received about my body size my entire life, and tries to "manage" my weight and my relationship to food by ripping my appearance to shreds or criticizing the food that I eat.

Carlos identified his most prominent manager part as his perfectionist part that stepped in to protect his exiled, younger parts. As a child, Carlos had to be the good immigrant kid, a star student, and be helpful with chores around the house. All the while, there were emotional parts of him holding feelings and memories from his traumatic separation from his parents, the sexual abuse that followed, and his immigration and peer rejection in the US as a Latino child in a small, white town. As a child he learned that in order to survive and make his parents both proud and less stressed out, he needed to push those big feeling parts away and "be good."

As an adult, Carlos still believed that if he was perfect, he would never receive any negative feedback that might trigger his younger parts. This is why managers manage—so that exiled, younger parts of us that hold pain, emotion, and trauma-related memories stay locked away out of consciousness, because that manager believes that younger part will totally overwhelm the system with their feelings. Or managers try to keep these younger parts safe from the world, from getting hurt again. Take a moment to ask yourself what manager parts you have. How do you keep yourself safe in this world, functioning, people pleasing, and protecting your child parts?

Then, there are firefighters. They are protectors whose purpose is to extinguish extreme pain or nervous system overwhelm, no matter the cost. We can think of this like a firefighter coming into a burning house: They aren't going to take stock of what's inside to avoid getting valuables wet. They are going to put out the fire no matter what gets damaged along the way. The "fire hose" could be filled with alcohol, drugs, binging or purging, self-harm, overexercising, dissociating, and extreme overworking. At some point in my life, I have used every single one of these. Most of my clients have too. We choose the medicine that fits the pain, and when we are in a lot of pain, we need a strong medicine! What are your go-to firefighters? What firefighters have you utilized in the past?

When Carlos was far outside his window of tolerance, his firefighter would take over and turn on the dissociation hose, and suddenly he wasn't overwhelmed. He wasn't feeling anything at all.

Meet Your Exiles

Exiles are kind of like the inner child Jung proposed in his work on archetypes. According to Jung, the young parts of ourselves hold our emotions and memories—both good and traumatic. But there is often more than one single inner child. As we learned above, our protectors believe that these emotions and memories will overwhelm the system and we won't be able to function because of the pain. Our protectors' mission is "Not again," and they do everything they can to protect these younger, vulnerable parts from any more pain or trauma. Think of Rapunzel locked away in the tower. She was put there to be protected, but she was cut off from the rest of the world. Protection meant banishment. This is what happens to our exiles.

Carlos could identify two exiles—the six-year-old abandoned and abused child, and the teen part of himself who strived to be the perfect student and struggled to build peer relationships as one of the only kids of color at his school. This latter part held a belief—"There is something wrong with me"—and felt the sharp pain of rejection. Carlos had put the child and teen parts of himself away in hopes of surviving and finding acceptance. They were exiled, banished from the rest of the internal family, because they hold big feelings, trauma memories, wounds from childhood. What exiled parts do you have? One way to think of this is the inner child and the inner teen, like Carlos did.

Meet Your Self

At the center of the protection parts and exiles is the core Self, our own inner loving parent.

What makes Self different from other parts is that it actually isn't a part. Self is our true essence. Our soul, even. Self contains, according to IFS, Self-energy, the power and ability to create inner wholeness and cohesion through healing, and, I would argue, a new attachment experience for our parts. In IFS therapy it is not the therapist but the Self that creates change, that allows burdened parts to let go of their pain and heal.

IFS defines the Self using the eight C's: *compassion*, *curiosity*, *clarity*, *creativity*, *calm*, *confidence*, *courage*, and *connectedness*. When we are in Self, we feel these qualities. When we have an agenda, some kind of goal or outcome outside of feeling more whole, or don't feel curious or compassionate about ourselves, we are not in Self, we are not being a loving parent toward our younger selves. Another part is driving the bus of our experience.

These eight aspects of Self are what make it different from protectors or exiles. When our protective parts run the show—managing or firefighting—we are not connected with ourselves, our body, or other people. When exiles run the show, we are emotionally and physically overwhelmed. We don't feel calm, confident, or courageous. But when Self runs the show, we are regulated, grounded, connected, compassionate, and ready to be the inner loving parent needed for our parts.

Remember our old friend attachment theorist Donald Winnicott from the previous chapter? Our True Self, according to him, our Self-energy in IFS, is who we are at our core, not what others need us to be.

YOUR TURN

How Do You Define Your True Self?

What does Self feel like in your body? When and how have you felt True?

Take a moment to scan your memory for an experience where you felt the most yourself. This might be an experience from childhood or from recent memory. If you are having a hard time finding a memory, I suggest looking back through old or recent photos and videos. Was there a past or recent experience where you can recall feeling compassionate, curious, clear, creative, calm, confident, courageous, and connected? Those eight C's are how IFS defines the Self, but what are your words? What words define your True Self?

Now, when you bring that memory into your mind's eye, what feelings do you notice? What do you notice in your body, any sensations, and where are those sensations located?

My client Jessy, who we met in chapter 1, experiences Self in pole class. Jessy found that she could break the cycle of dissociation of Netflix binging in the evenings by stopping by the pole studio on the way home from work. The studio was a supportive environment, a place for her to safely express and explore her femininity. Being on the pole requires her to be in her body. When Jessy watches videos on her phone that her friends at pole took of her doing certain tricks and routines, she smiles with pride. "That's who I really am," she told me one day, sharing a video of a new routine. "That's Jessy."

I have always found my Self by recalling memories where I

felt the most Andrea, the most connected to who I truly am at my core. These were experiences where I felt the most at home in my body, closest to my essence of *me*.

For me, being in Self always makes my body feel like a wind tunnel, like there is endless room for air. My body feels open and free. When not in Self, I feel as though my body is crowded and gunked up, as if my core Self is covered in sticky mud and all my parts that are in pain or trying to overcompensate by micromanaging are stuck to my core. I feel sluggish and unable to move freely in my thoughts and in my body.

What do you feel when you are not in Self?

The process of separating all those parts from Self—clearing the way for Self to shine—is called the unblending process. Unblending is a way to declutter the Self so that you can feel compassionate, curious, clear, creative, calm, confident, courageous, and connected.

But before you can unblend parts, you need to identify them. Let's look at how Carlos was able to recognize his inner parts so he could get back to Self being the driver of his experience.

MOVING FROM A PARTS-LED MINDSET TO A SELF-LED MINDSET

Of Carlos's two protector parts, his perfectionist part ran the show 90 percent of the time. This part believed that if he was absolutely perfect both professionally and in his relationships, no one would notice he was an immigrant, gay, and a person of color. This part of him held his anxiety and believed he was keeping his younger parts safe, which in some ways was true, but at the same time this part was keeping him from his authenticity. When we are perfect, we can't be human. Carlos wasn't able to tap into the safety of his current life because his protectors were running the show. It kept him in survival mode. When Carlos was overwhelmed, the furthest outside of his window of tolerance, his dissociation firefighter part took over his body and helped him to leave it. This part ran the show about 10 percent of the time, when shit got really bad. He would find himself watching his body move through the day, as if he were perched in a corner of the ceiling and not inside of his body. When this part took over, he didn't feel overwhelmed. He felt completely disconnected. This part is how Carlos survived being separated from his parents and helped him survive the sexual abuse. When he missed his parents, or when his abuser was harming him, he would leave his body to varying degrees.

Once Carlos had identified his protective and exiled parts, he was ready to get to know them using an exercise called Driving the Bus. When our True Self is in the driver's seat, we make choices we feel good about, we feel embodied, and we feel authentic. But when our nervous system detects a threat—and for those of us on the margins this can be daily—protectors swoop in to keep us safe, and when they get control of the bus, our Self can get pushed to the back. When a protector is running the show, exiles tend to get exiled to the back of the bus too—"No time for feeling, gotta get to safety!" Or protectors believe those tender, wounded parts of us would be safest relegated to the back so they don't see what's going on up front. When a protector is driving the bus—and for many of us, this is most of the time—we feel disconnected from our core Self.

One day, Carlos came into our session with a conflict he needed help resolving. Jon, his boyfriend, wanted Carlos to come with him to his cousin's wedding that weekend. Jon's family, however, did not accept Jon's queerness. They referred to Carlos as Jon's roommate. Also, Jon is white, as is his family, and they had made racist comments in the past, such as remarking on "how good" Carlos's English is. Jon's mother shocked Carlos by saying how "smart he is for an illegal immigrant." Obviously, being around Jon's family was going to be very triggering for Carlos, and he wanted to work through whether or not he should go to the wedding.

I asked Carlos to close his eyes and invite his parts forward. He noticed right away who was driving the bus. It was not his core Self. It was his people-pleasing perfectionist part, and it was telling all of the other parts on the bus to suck it up and go along to the wedding because it was what Jon wanted. Being the perfect boyfriend would mean going to the wedding, even though it meant his core Self and all of his parts were going to feel disrespected by Jon's family's racist and homophobic behavior.

I asked Carlos, "And who's sitting right behind the driver's seat?"

It was the firefighter—his dissociation part. This part was ready to take over at the wedding so that Carlos wouldn't have to hear the dehumanizing comments and could just leave his body, not feeling pain.

"What other parts do you notice on the bus and where are they?" I asked.

Carlos noticed that toward the back of the bus were his exiled parts: that teen part that feared peer rejection and that child self who felt abandoned by his parents and endured sexual abuse. The teen was really scared not to go to the wedding. He was filled with anxiety and fear of disappointing Jon if he refused to go. He worried he would be rejected all over again. He was also afraid of failure if he did go—if he didn't please Jon's family at the wedding, that might result in rejection too. Being rejected by the man he loved, the person who saw and understood him more than anyone else in the world, was an overwhelming thought.

His child self didn't want to go to the wedding and was worried about being trapped in a room with strangers, unable to leave. This part had been through so much—had in fact been trapped in a room with hostile strangers many times before. He just wanted to run away and hide.

Now that we had heard from all his parts, Carlos didn't have the answer to what to do about the wedding quite yet, but he started to feel his core Self taking over his body and thoughts instead of all of these separate parts.

Carlos was able to make a decision in his core Self to show up and care for his teen and child parts instead of letting a protector or exile make choices for him about what to do next. Carlos did not attend the wedding and spent the weekend resting and hanging out with friends. His partner was disappointed, but they were able to work through that together as a couple because Jon ultimately understood. After all, as a gay man whose family didn't acknowledge his sexuality and partnership, Jon's own exiles could relate! But it takes good communication for couples to understand where decisions that affect them both are coming from.

Being Self-led is hard. For me, even after all of the work I have done on myself, my manager parts tend to run the show and I have to work hard to get my Self back in the driver's seat. It usually takes extended time away from work and home—going hiking or camping—to get my Self back in control. When I am in the woods, there is no task left to do, no calendar to look at. I can finally be Self-led instead of manager-led. But I can't live my life in the woods. Plus, I deeply love what I do, and without my work, I would feel pretty empty and out of Self.

So how can I experience Self outside of that safe space of nature? How do any of us locate Self when we get caught up in the day-to-day managing or firefighter-led survival? Let's explore the answer together. In a moment, you'll do the Driving the Bus exercise yourself, but first, let's get to know your parts.

GET TO KNOW YOUR PARTS

If you are manager-led, you tend to:

- Be a perfectionist and high achiever
- Be self-critical
- Be self-protective: "I don't need other people"
- Get anxious or stuck in your head
- Have difficulty accessing emotions
- Enjoy task completion
- People please
- Need other people to see you as good and capable
- Ignore your own feelings and focus on others'
- Want or need other people to be okay
- Feel like people don't see your pain
- Have had to manage family members as a child, parentified in some way
- Feel like there is a wall between you and the rest of the world

What about those who are firefighter-led? If this is you, you tend to:

- Use drinking, drugs, disordered eating, and self-harm to deal with big, overwhelming feelings
- Be extremely checked out, dissociated, or numbed out
- Overwork to the point of severe physical or emotional harm
- Have difficulty regulating emotions or feeling grounded
- Have trouble concentrating
- Go from extremely anxious to extremely depressed
- Feel disconnected from others unless you are drinking or using with them

And then there are those who are exile-led. Your protective system isn't really able to keep these younger, emotional parts locked away, and they end up driving the bus a lot of the time. Think about a child driving a bus, how scary and overwhelming that would be. If you are exile-led, you tend to:

- Have tearful or crying spells
- Feel hopelessness, panic, and fear
- Be highly sensitive
- Have low self-esteem
- Experience frequent PTSD or cPTSD symptoms: intrusive images, nightmares, emotional flashbacks, feeling like the bad thing is happening all over again
- Feel desperate for someone to see your pain and care for you

Now, I don't know many people who are Self-led most of the time. I find healing and growth to be less about being Self-led and more about being able to identify what part is driving the bus, like Carlos did, and then being able to unblend with that part and come back to Self.

When we are connected to Self we feel:

- Inside our bodies, connected to our breath, and our feet on the ground
- Physically and emotionally calm, or able to handle big feelings by feeling them
- Able to tolerate feelings or distress in our bodies without numbing them by dissociating, scrolling, using drugs and alcohol, et cetera
- Authentic, like our core Self can shine through
- Connected to other people and the world around us
- Curious about ourselves and the world
- Able to express our creativity

You may read the above and feel like you can be all of these parts in one single day. The reality is that our parts make up our internal family, so they are all there all of the time. My goal is to help you understand who shows up most of the time or what it can look or feel like when these parts show up. Maybe you can't identify which of these parts leads you, but by practicing the Driving the Bus exercise and focusing on how your body feels, you will begin to be able to identify your parts. This awareness is going to help you recognize what situations they show up in.

I've noticed that my clients who are manager-, firefighter-, and/or exile-led hold a lot of shame about showing up in the world in this way. For clients who are more manager-led, there is shame about being cut off from their emotions, struggling to feel close to other people, and about being "cold." For those who are more firefighter-led, there is shame about being "too much," shame about utilizing more extreme coping mechanisms, shame about being "a mess." Exile-led folks tend to find themselves in situations where they are being manipulated and harmed for just breadcrumbs of love, attention, and affection.

All of our parts have good intentions. Whoever drives the bus of your experience most of the time has been doing so to try to keep you safe or get your needs met in any way possible. Our parts picked up these ways of dealing with big feelings, trauma, and daily life for a reason. But we can help our parts find other ways of getting our needs met and feeling relief.

YOUR TURN

Who Is Driving Your Bus?

Let's take a deeper look at who is driving your bus most of the time. This is the part of you that leads most of your day-to-day experience.

One good way to get to know your parts is to pay attention when you have a stressful decision to make. Scan your mind for a minor inner conflict in your life. Don't choose something trauma-related or triggering for now. It's okay if a traumatic conflict comes up; you can always use your Container and Safe Place (see chapters 1 and 2) to ground yourself and save the heavy content to talk about with your therapist, sponsor, or a safe loved one later. Sometimes "minor" issues lead to bigger stuff, and if that feels okay, just go with it. Make sure to check in with your body to sense whether you are inside your window of tolerance (see chapter 1) or if you need some containment (chapter 2).

The most common type of inner conflict I hear is "part of me wants or thinks this and another part of me wants or feels something totally different." This can look like "should I stay or should I go?" in a job, city, or relationship.

Once you've identified your inner conflict, notice which parts show up and who needs to be heard first.

The point of this exercise is not to find the right answer to your conflict. It's to hear from all your parts so you can better understand how your core Self feels about the conflict. This practice is meant to help you unblend and allow all of your parts to exist while also connecting to your Self once again.

We do this exercise by checking in with all parts. Simply

doing this stimulates the unblending process, making more room for Self to get back into the driver's seat.

Listen to the different opinions that arise internally. Sometimes it helps to write them down or sketch them out as they come up. Imagine or even draw the bus and which part is sitting where and what they have to say. Remember, the point of this exercise is not to come to a definite conclusion. It's important to have no agenda when working with parts other than to hear them out.

Ask yourself these questions to find out more about your parts:

What do you notice inside your body when you think of this inner conflict? What sensations and tension do you notice? What parts of your body light up when you drop in?

Who is driving the bus of this inner conflict? As in, whose voice is the loudest? Whose voice is being followed or listened to the most? Is it your Self who is in the driver's seat, or another part? If it's another part, what do you want to call this part? You might call it "the angry part" or "the frightened part" or "the insecure part." Is this part you at a certain age, like "teenage me" or "little Andrea"? Or is it a protective part that wants to reach for the fire hose or a part that wants to be in charge and control the outcome?

Who sits right behind that bus driver? Or maybe this is a part that is battling it out at the steering wheel, trying to take control. What is their name?

Who's behind these parts? Voices a little quieter but still present? Name these parts too.

Now go even deeper inward. *Who is at the back of the bus not being seen or listened to at all?* What do you want to call these parts? What do they think about this inner conflict?

What happens to how you feel about this conflict when you hear from all of these parts?

What do you feel in your body now that you have heard from everyone? How is it the same or different from how you felt at the start of the exercise?

Without feeling any pressure to have an answer to the inner conflict, *how do you feel toward the conflict now?*

Working with Protectors—the Six F's

If your protector parts are driving your bus, you aren't alone. They often occupy our drivers' seats. The goal of parts work is to have your Self in the driver's seat, but protectors can't just be booted out. Protectors want to be understood, as well as honored for the role they have been serving. They can't be forced into a new role; they have to be invited. If I said to my client Carlos, "Just stop trying to be so perfect all the time. Perfection is impossible. Let that standard go. It isn't serving you," I would be pushing past his perfectionist manager, rejecting that part of him, and not honoring the role it has served his system.

Instead, we can use a method called the six F's to work with protectors[13] and get them to take on a new job within the internal family system. Let's look at the six F's together.

Find: This is where we choose the protector part we want to work with. There are a few different ways to do that. We can locate a part simply by turning our attention inward and asking, "Who needs to be heard first?" We can encourage our parts to speak up by identifying an inner conflict, like we did above. We can also find a part by checking in with a sensation in our body, scanning the body and noticing where we feel tension, warmth, tingling, or any other sensation. These sensations are usually parts. For Carlos, he feels his dissociation firefighter part show up as a numbing sensation in his hands, that spreads to his whole body as he checks out. His exile always showed up as a lump in his throat, and a sinking sensation in his gut.

Focus: Now that you have found the part you want to work with, what happens when you focus on it? What do you notice about this part? What does it look like? What qualities does it hold? When Carlos and I were practicing the Driving the Bus exercise, he noticed his dissociation firefighter part showing up to cut him off from the pain of being exposed to his boyfriend's family. This part appeared to Carlos as a black pit that sucked down all of his negative emotions before he could feel them, leaving him feeling nothing. Carlos noticed that when he focused on the part, it didn't like being noticed. It liked being unseen.

Flesh out: What's the difference between this part of you and your True Self? Flesh out that difference. What role does this part serve? Is this an exile or a protector? How old were you when this part formed? Is this part a child? A teen? An adult? Carlos's dissociation part formed when his parents left for the US and only strengthened when the sexual abuse began. This part protected his exiled child part, the one that held the emotional overwhelm and fear of abandonment and abuse.

Feel toward: This is your Self meeting the part. How do you feel toward this part of yourself? How does the part feel toward you? If you feel very negatively toward this part, see if the part of you that feels negatively can take one step back in the bus and unblend from Self to make room for some love and compassion for the target part. Continue this process until you are able to feel some love and connection toward the target part, until you have unblended from all parts that block you from loving this part of you. At first Carlos was frustrated with his dissociation firefighter, which clued him in that there was another part present. His frustration at his dissociation part stemmed from the perfectionist, who saw dissociation as getting in the way of being fully healed and therefore perfect. Carlos asked his perfectionist part to take a step back so he could feel toward his dissociation part from a place of Self. This process took many sessions, as his perfectionist part was really blocking Carlos from feeling compassionate toward his dissociation part. Once his perfectionist did step back, Carlos was able to feel a lot of love and appreciation for dissociation. "I know without my dissociation part, I could have never survived my childhood."

Be**friend**: Validate the part's role and why it had to take it on. Honor what it has done for you. You can even imagine holding this part's hand or going to sit down next to it. During our befriending session, Carlos imagined sitting with his dissociation part by the beach, his Safe Place. He set up a blanket with snacks, books, and pillows in his mind's eye, and asked if the part would be willing to sit with him there for a while, take a load off. Carlos told the part, "I see all you have done and are doing for me to survive—you must be exhausted."

Explore **fears**: Why did this part take on this extreme role? Ask what it fears would happen if it let go of this protective role. Does it want a new role, and if so, what would that be? What would this part want to do with its time and energy if it no longer had to protect you? See if this part would be willing to let you, your True Self, fulfill this role, even if it's just for a day, or for a minute. How would this part spend this time if it trusted your Self to keep you safe? Carlos's dissociation part told him that it took on the protector role so Carlos would not die—that he would not die without his parents, but also would submit to his abuser and not risk fighting back and being hurt or killed. This is why the part had been so unwilling to let Carlos's Self run the show; it truly believed that Carlos would die if it stopped protecting him. The dissociation part told Carlos, "I am so tired. If I were to have a new role, it would be to rest. To make sure you rest too."

YOUR TURN

Working with Your Protectors

Like Carlos, go through the six F's above to learn about your protectors. Invite them to take on a new role. It can be really helpful to journal through this exercise, writing observations from the perspective of the protector part of you, as well as from any other protector parts that speak up. Some people like to use the six F's as a meditation practice, and many IFS therapists have uploaded guided meditations online for this practice. You can also bring this exercise to your therapy, to your work with your sponsor, or to your own meditation practice. If at any point this process feels dysregulating, stop and go to your Safe Place or use your Container. This process of the six F's is absolutely something you can do on your own, but it should never be dysregulating. If it is, you may need more of a guided environment to do it in, like therapy or your step work.

After you've worked through the six F's with your protector, see if there is enough trust between you and your protector to explore who this part is trying to save. You can simply ask the part, "Who are you protecting?" or you can see by checking in with your mind and body if any younger parts—any exiles—have shown up. If at any point you feel out of your window of tolerance, return to your Safe Place, put any distressing content, feelings, or images in your Container, and wait to keep processing until you are with a therapist, sponsor, or trusted person in your life. If you feel ready, you can speak to your exile.

Working with Your Exiles

Your exile is the part that the protector has been keeping safe, or has been scared it would overwhelm your system if it showed up. Carlos learned that his protector parts were shielding his frightened child self. Now that he had a sense of who his protector was protecting, it was time to *unburden* his exiled part.

There are five steps to inviting your exile to speak: witness, do over, retrieve, unburden, and integrate. Together, let's explore each one with Carlos:

Witness: Ask the exile to show you whatever it needs you, the Self, to know. It might show you an image of a memory, or of the part itself suffering. See its pain, its memories, how it became exiled in the first place. For Carlos, once his dissociation had stepped back and taken on the new role of the "the one who rests," he was ready to meet his exile: his terrified, lonely, hurt child self. The part came to him with an image of a little boy in a room, alone, curled up in the corner, crying. Carlos's adult Self went and joined the exile in the room, telling the part, "I am with you, and I see your pain."

Do Over: Create a mismatch with the exile. Go back into the memory your exile showed you and allow something different to happen. What did it need then that it didn't get? Give your exile that missing experience! Carlos had found his child exile in his old childhood bedroom at his extended family's home. First, in the witness phase, he introduced himself to this scared child as the safe, constantly present, protective adult that his child self had so needed. Now the do-over can happen. Carlos asked the scared, lonely part, "Do you want to come with me? To a better place?" The exile nodded and Carlos took his little hand.

Retrieve: Bring the exile out of the past memory into the present. If you are already in the present, invite this part of you to stay here with you now instead of going back to the past. Maybe you want to show them where there is space for them in your life, in your home, in your healing journey. In this step, Carlos showed his exile his life now, including his safe, warm home with his partner Jon and their dogs, and Jon's love and care for Carlos. He gave his exile their bright, airy guest room and showed the child part how close this room was to his and Jon's. He told the exile, "We will be here whenever you need us. I'm not going anywhere, I am here to protect you now."

Unburden: Ask the exile what it wants to let go of. What have you been carrying that you want to release? These burdens could be negative beliefs, overwhelming body sensations, unseen emotions. Where does the exile want to release them to? This tends to be somewhere in nature—think air, water, earth, or fire. What element would allow them to release this burden best? Now that his exile felt safe in Carlos's adult home, it wanted to release the fear of being harmed and the grief of being left. The exile brought these emotions to the fireplace in Carlos's den and made a fire to release these burdens together.

Integrate: Invite the protector to witness what the exile has unburdened. See if the protector is ready to accept a new role now that the exile has let go of what it has been carrying and has a safe home in the present reality. This new role might just be resting or allowing themselves to be the child they never were. These roles don't have to be functional ones. When I do this step with clients, the most common role the protector wants is to not have a job at all and instead to be free. Dissociation and the perfectionist joined Carlos and his exile in the den to watch the trauma burn away in the fireplace. Carlos imagined himself putting his arm around his child self and felt dissociation and perfectionism melt away into the background, going to their own Safe Places to rest and fulfill their new roles in his system.

As Carlos and I built an inner sense of community among all these parts, Carlos became less scared of his child and teen selves who had experienced life-threatening traumas and peer rejection. He learned to sit with these parts of himself, befriending them and holding space for their fears and needs. His perfectionist and dissociation parts don't take over his body as often, and when they do, he is able to notice that he is no longer in Self. Now he himself sits at the center of his experience, his core, authentic Self, tending to his child parts and protecting other parts as they arise.

YOUR TURN

Unburden Your Exiles

Like Carlos, go through the unburdening process above. Work through all five steps to invite your exile to speak. Your exile may not have been heard from in a long time, if ever. Most of us have more than one exile, so make sure you go slowly and work with one at a time, allowing each to be deeply heard. As with the six F's process, if at any part of this the work feels dysregulating or overwhelming, please save it to do with your therapist or another trusted person in your life. I suggest getting out a notebook and journaling throughout this process or imagining it in your mind's eye with meditation.

Witness: This is where you allow the exile you are going to work with to come forward and make themselves known. How do they appear to you? What age are they? Allow them to show you themselves, their pain, what they have been through.

Do Over: This is where you offer the exile a new experience. Using your adult Self, your inner loving parent, offer your exile love, compassion, nurturance, protection, and guidance where they did not receive it. Maybe you rescue them from an unsafe situation. Maybe you sit with them and listen when no one else has. Examples of missing experiences could be any of the following:

- Going to where the exile is or has been since being exiled. You might even say, "You are not alone anymore" or "I see you now."
- Getting the exile out of a trauma memory and bringing it somewhere safe.
- Noticing where the exile is in the body (where we feel that part or feel its pain) and bringing our hand there. This can be combined with a statement like "I'm here with you" or seeing if the exile can sense your loving touch.
- Visualizing taking the hand of the exile in yours. Hold, rock, hug this exile.
- Having the exile sense the protection of your adult body, or even sharing a statement like "I'm here to protect you."[14]

Retrieve: Update this part about what life is like now. Bring them into the present. Show them the life you have made. Even if you aren't 100 percent happy with your life, or even 50 percent, remember that for this part, the fact that you are in control even a little bit of your adult life is a huge deal to this younger part that had no power. The fact that they have *you* to love and care for them is a very big deal. Show them your life now, all the ways you have grown and changed, all the ways life is safer now than it was then.

Unburden: This is where the exile gets to let go of their trauma and the burdens that were put on them. Ask them where they want to release this burden and be with them for that process. Is there somewhere in your Safe Place they would like to let go of these feelings, beliefs, sensations? Maybe they want to store them in your Container. Or is there somewhere in nature they want to release their burden into?

Integrate: Invite the protector you worked with during your six F's to take in the unburdened exile. What is it like for this protector to see that the exile has released this trauma, this burden? Ask the protector what it would like to do now that they don't have to spend all their time protecting.

The Adult Children of Alcoholics and Dysfunctional Families (ACA) approach to parts work is to focus on the parts as an inner family. Two of these inner family members are the inner critical parent and an inner loving parent. You might want to try the following exercises, phrasing the relationships of your inner parts in this way.[15]

The Inner Critic

Your inner critic, also known as an inner critical parent, may be trying to protect you from something: danger, external criticism, rejection, failure, and so on. However, the inner critic replicates your hurt and pain, criticizing you in ways that are all too familiar. If you notice that you have an inner critical parent, start working with this part by identifying the way you speak to yourself. Are you critical, lacking kindness, rigid, or harsh when you speak to yourself? The inner critical parent can show up in the body as muscle tension and restricted breathing. You can place a hand on your chest, or anywhere else you feel that tension, and simply say, "This isn't me, this is my inner critical parent." Many of my clients then imagine themselves as little kids or as teens, or even imagine another child in their life. Would they speak to that little kid the way they just spoke to themselves? The answer is always no.

YOUR TURN

Meeting Your Inner Critical Parent

How do you speak to yourself when your inner critical parent is driving the bus?

Do these statements remind you of anyone in your life, or any lessons you were taught by the world?

What is the mental image that comes to mind when you imagine your inner critical parent?

How would you speak to your little kid self instead? What kind words did you need to hear that you didn't get as a child?

The Inner Loving Parent

The balm to our inner critical parent is another interpretation of our core Self—our inner loving parent. This is the *compassionate, calm, curious* parent so few of us got as children. This inner loving parent cares for our inner parts just like a loving parent would. They protect, nurture, guide, and support.

Many of my clients step into Self best when they think of themselves as the kind, sturdy caregiver to their inner parts. This creates immense compassion for parts that they typically would feel critical toward. Imagining becoming this inner loving parent is another way to differentiate your Self from your inner critical parent and invite self-compassion. So let's meet yours.

YOUR TURN

Meeting Your Inner Loving Parent

As above, imagine a child in your life, whether it be your own, the child of your partner, a dear friend, a sibling, or even imagine any kid you see on the playground or at the grocery store. Now imagine what you would say to this child if they made a mistake or felt sad or overwhelmed. What did you need to hear as a child but never did? What image comes to mind when you imagine being the inner loving parent to this child? Now imagine *yourself* as a child, meeting an adult you.

What does it feel like to embody this idea of being the mama bear, papa bear, or fierce protector of your little kid parts? How might that change your inner dialogue with yourself and the boundaries you put in place?

So much of who we are—in all our parts—is the result of all that we have learned together in the book so far: how trauma affects our nervous systems, how our brains were impacted by trauma, and how our caregiver relationships shaped our connections with others and ourselves. It also goes deeper than that—sometimes as deep as our genes. In IFS, one of the burdens a part can take on is called a legacy burden, which we will explore together in chapter 7. This type of burden doesn't always fit with the reality of our life today, but it feels in our bodies as though it does.

BRINGING IT ALL TOGETHER

Parts work gives us the experience of healing our internal attachment to ourselves. We can unburden and befriend our inner parts and invite our protector parts to step back from their roles of shielding our frightened exiled parts. We can use Self-energy to validate, witness, and heal our parts; we can give ourselves what we so rarely get in society and many of us didn't receive at home with our caregivers. These experiences create mismatches, which allow our brain and attachment system to have a corrective emotional experience. This is exactly how we rewire our brains and nervous systems after trauma, after childhoods where we had to hide our True Self.

In the next chapter, we will apply all the skills and theories we have learned over the first half of the book to often-unrecognized traumas that most of us experience every day.

PART 3

UNDERSTANDING AND HEALING FROM *YOUR* TRAUMA

CHAPTER 5

Healing from Oppression-Based Trauma

We've learned about how the nervous system responds to trauma and stress; how the brain creates new pathways for healing; how our early attachment experiences impact our lives; and how to accept and befriend our parts. Now we'll look at how we can teach ourselves to feel safe, to create new experiences, and to heal from the traumas that often get neglected, unseen, or ignored. The unseen trauma we will explore together in this chapter is oppression-based trauma. Oppression *is* trauma in its expression in our daily lives, but it also lives and breathes within our bodies, within the very foundation of our society, and even in the rapid destruction of our planet.

Oppression makes us feel existential danger because this source of trauma is everywhere. But in this chapter, I'll show you how you can discover your sense of safety and of self by creating mismatches within those three core branches of healing: community, freedom, and compassion.

OPPRESSION

What do I mean by *oppression*?

We encounter oppression through micro- and macroexperiences. Microexperiences of oppression are "everyday" moments of witnessing or being the target of racism, homophobia or transphobia, ableism, and so on. It can be an insulting comment by someone at work or on the subway. It can be arriving at work to discover the automatic door is still broken. It can be someone refusing to use your pronouns. These experiences aren't called micro because they are small and don't matter. They are micro in the sense that they occur so frequently that they degrade us bit by bit, in ways that deteriorate our sense of self—yet we are gaslit to downplay their damaging impact. We are told to just "get over" the insult or that we are "making too big a deal out of" being unseen.

Macroexperiences of oppression are big and inescapable: Living every day in a society that doesn't believe sexual assault survivors. Not having access to basic and lifesaving medical care because of fatphobia. Worrying whether we can make rent because our job doesn't pay us a living wage. Having to care for a sick parent because they have lived next to a coal mine all their lives.

These ongoing stressful experiences are deeply linked to systemic oppression. We can only experience ease and calm if we have our basic needs met and feel safe in the world. Macro-oppression is baked into systems like capitalism, corporate health care, the education system, the prison-industrial complex, and others. As activist and scholar Angela Davis wisely said, "Colonialism and slavery were the foundations of capitalism."[1] We can't talk about the oppressive nature of capitalism without talking about how capitalism was created by white European colonizers. They believed it was their God-given right to take land away from, enslave, traumatize, and murder millions. Extractive capitalism was born of this: Take what you want at any cost to other humans and Earth. Of course living in these conditions—especially if you hold minimal power or privilege—is stressful, and therefore traumatizing. Major life traumas are often deeply intertwined with oppressive systems.

Whether macro or micro, oppression causes stress, and stress activates our survival responses just like trauma does. Over time, repeated experiences of oppression flood our systems with stress hormones, which can result in chronic health problems. Or, through our fire hose of dissociation, they can shut us down, which is just as unhealthy for us. Our biggest, most impactful traumas in life—such as sexual assaults, frightening experiences with police, being unhoused, rejection from family—may intersect with an experience of oppression. Major life traumas that are related to oppression as well as everyday traumas that still set off our fight-or-flight response all need to be acknowledged and tended to.

In times of stress as well as rest, our brain's job is to allocate—or budget[2]—energy to different functions while keeping us safe, helping us maintain equilibrium. Trauma throws off our bodies' processes of balance. Energy is redirected away from long-term bodily needs—like healing and growth—and sent to tend to our immediate survival needs.[3] We get out of balance and live in survival mode. Long-term exposure to stress leads to trouble regulating emotions and a dysregulated nervous system.

When the body is not under extreme or ongoing stress or trauma, we are able to manage the ups and downs of life. We are able to cope with emotions and stressors and return to homeostasis (the body in balance internally, even as outside conditions change). We can feel safe, and our bodies recover from the day's demands. But many of us never get recovery time. We live in a constant state of oppression, which is why so many of us feel tired, dysregulated, emotionally exhausted, and are in chronic physical pain.

The less agency or control we feel during a trauma, the more actively traumatizing the incident is for our bodies. Traumas that are linked to oppression are always going to be experiences in which we feel powerless.[4]

The Effects of Oppression

My client Lindsey, in her late twenties, came to our work together with PTSD from a sexual assault when she was a teenager, one she was finally realizing impacted her immensely to this day.

Lindsey was assaulted by a doctor during an exam when she was sixteen. Together, we uncovered that a second trauma occurred for her when she was not believed by her parents or teachers about the sexual assault. Lindsey was a young Black woman, and both her race and her gender were held against her. Black women's pain has historically and statistically gone unacknowledged and invalidated by medical professionals. In fact, American gynecology as we know it today began as brutal experimentation on enslaved Black women by a doctor who did not use anesthesia during major surgeries.[5] We quite literally have OB-GYN care today because of the pain and torture of these women, and this is just one example of Black women's bodies being violated in the history of medical "progress."

Lindsey and I couldn't fully unpack her sexual trauma without exploring her experience of white supremacy and misogyny, a combination called misogynoir. It was traumatizing enough to be assaulted, but even more traumatizing to have her pain not taken seriously. Her trauma had left her feeling not human. And it wasn't the first time she had been made to feel this way.

In the years before the assault, Lindsey would spend hours reading the *DSM*, trying to find out what was "wrong" with her after experiencing big emotions and deep, existential loneliness at a young age. She had always felt like she was defective in some way.

And so, in therapy, in healing from the sexual assault, Lindsey also needed to tend to her lifelong experience of racial and gendered trauma.

In order to be successful in her job as a social media director, Lindsey had learned to become someone tolerable, digestible in her all-white workplace. She didn't have a name for it as a child, but as an adult she recognized what she was doing was code-switching: the act of shifting between an authentic presentation of self and, in Lindsey's case, a whitewashed self, devoid of culture. She felt an enormous fissure in her life between who she really was and who the world needed her to be.

Clinical psychologist Jennifer Mullan writes, "colonization is a psychological and spiritual trauma."[6] Colonization—and the enslavement born from it—lives on in the bodies and psyche of every single person whose lands were stolen from them, whose ancestors were forced into enslavement.

Lindsey and I worked together processing her trauma of code-switching—how she behaved, how she dressed, and how she held herself were all determined by who she was around. She had been doing this for so long that she actually had no idea what she wanted to wear, how she wanted to speak, what she wanted from her life, or even who she really was.

We also dug into her family culture. She had been raised to leave her Blackness behind when she left her house: stiff, uncomfortable, with a knot in her stomach, dressed in clothes intended as camouflage, erasing anything about her that expressed her culture and identity. It was the opposite of the self-expression through appearance that most teens are drawn to. In fact, she had been raised to suppress self-expression because to her community and family, the expression of culture had been demonized. This was how she and her family stayed safe in a world of police racism, being constantly under the threat of stop-and-frisk in New York City, and how they had stayed safe for generations. This hypervigilance had shown up in her body as a child and in her early teens as different medical issues, hormone imbalances, and insomnia. After the sexual assault, these only got worse.

What we also discovered was that Lindsey had been experiencing PTSD symptoms long before her assault. Even as a young child she had felt hypervigilant, fragmented, and cut off from the rest of the world. Before anything "really bad" had happened to her, she had been living with the pressure and stress of oppression, and it wasn't until getting trauma therapy as an adult for the assault that she uncovered a lifetime of oppression-based trauma.

Our trauma is a complex web, and interwoven into that web are threads of historical traumas that impact many of us to this day. Recently, thanks to the work of therapists who are queer, trans, and POC, as well as antiracist and decolonial, the impact of oppression-based trauma is starting to be acknowledged by the field of psychotherapy—trauma psychotherapy in particular. This means the field is beginning to recognize the impacts of racism, colonialism, homophobia, transphobia, ableism, classism, social and environmental injustice, and other forms of oppression on our nervous system, sense of self, and health, just as it acknowledges other traumatic experiences like car accidents, assault, natural disasters, and war. We cannot fully heal from trauma without seeing how intertwined it is with these cultural burdens.

Lindsey often says that rape culture and white supremacy is the soup we are all cooked in. She wasn't able to process her sexual assault until she also processed the reality of growing up in a society where she had already been raised to believe that her body was something to be concealed and made acceptable to a white world. She felt that if anything bad happened to her, it must be her fault because she had failed at that task.

Many of my clients come to our work with trauma that is compounded by an oppressive system and cultural burdens. A number of clients and loved ones of mine who are BIPOC have experienced sexual assault but believed they could not report it because they felt the "justice" system not only was not for them but was actually dangerous for them. Living in a police state as a person of color is stressful and unsafe, every day. Living in an ableist society for my chronically ill and disabled clients is traumatizing and life-threatening, every day. Living in a queer and/or trans body in a transphobic/homophobic society is invalidating and often terrifying, every day. The list goes on.

HOW DO WE HEAL?

What is the opposite of oppression? What experience creates the most impactful mismatch for our bodies and parts that are suffering from oppression?

Liberation.

Liberation psychology originated in Latin America through the work of social psychologist Ignacio Martín-Baró. This school of thought is dedicated to both acknowledging the major impact of oppression on our mental health and creating experiences for marginalized peoples to experience freedom, happiness, and a sense of ownership over their bodies and lives.[7] Liberation psychology also reminds us that psychology itself needs to be liberated. Just as the therapeutic space has not always been safe for queer and trans folks, people of color, neurodivergent people, and others, psychology itself is incredibly Eurocentric. Healing is always viewed as linear. The goal of psychology in a capitalist system is not really healing but rather functioning better to be a better worker.

Liberation psychology, born out of a culture of collectivism, pushes back against the individualism of the US and Europe, arguing that we can't heal without collective liberation. We cannot fully liberate ourselves from oppression through individual work alone. The individual psychotherapy session is merely one realm—of many—where healing can occur. Liberation psychology asks us to decolonize our views of healing, allowing other non-Western approaches to be as valid and effective as "evidence-based" practices. It also acknowledges that people who come from colonized and enslaved lineages cannot heal without healing the trauma of colonization itself. Most important for people on the margins, liberation psychology emphasizes that any individual liberation leads to the liberation of the collective[8]—that *none of us is free until all of us are free.*

This idea is the foundation of trauma healing for the oppressed body. Our individual healing has a ripple effect throughout our family and friend networks, extending into our communities. We need to move away from healing individually in little rooms, and rather think of any action, including psychotherapy, we take toward a more just world to be our healing, our liberation.[9]

Liberation work itself is anything that moves us and the collective toward liberation from oppression. So what does healing together from oppression look like?

Now we will really dig into the three core principles of trauma healing for people on the margins, for all oppressed people—community, freedom, and compassion—because they are our biggest mismatches to oppression-based trauma. We heal from oppression-based trauma in community. We heal when our oppressed body feels freedom. We heal when we feel compassion for ourselves and honor our authenticity through being safe and loved for who we are in all our identities.

In the following sections, we'll explore community through mutual aid, access intimacy, and sharing spaces. We'll experience freedom through dance, nature, sex, body mod, gender-affirming care, art, activism. And we'll remember to feel compassion for ourselves through tending to our wounded and rejected parts, allowing ourselves to be authentic.

HEALING IN COMMUNITY

Healing Through Mutual Aid

Mutual aid is the radical act of sharing resources and support without reproducing the colonizer-colonized dynamic. Instead of nonprofit organizations donating money that was made on stolen land or using underpaid labor, community members share resources among themselves.[10] Hopefully, those with more resources share more, not for tax deductions or to appear generous but because they have it. Oftentimes, though, it's not even people with more access to resources who contribute. People give what they have, even if it's five dollars, and hope that if and when they need that support, they will get it too.

Mutual aid occurs quite often in my queer and trans community, where friends will throw fundraisers in person or online to raise money for someone's gender-affirming surgery, rent, car payment, or abortion, or even to bail someone out of jail when they are unable to pay a simple fine. I have seen these goals be met in a matter of hours by community members.

During the start and height of the COVID pandemic, micro-community groups popped up all over major cities, connecting neighbors with each other to meet basic needs gone unmet by the government and social services. In my old neighborhood in Brooklyn, an organization called Bed-Stuy Strong developed, where people could post in the group with their needs or skills they could offer others. An elderly person who was unable to get to the grocery store would have their list of items delivered within the hour from an able-bodied neighbor down the block. Someone too sick to leave their home could ask for a drugstore run, and someone who wasn't sick could take on the task and bring it to their doorstep. The group still exists, offering free local produce and hosting events to meet your neighbors and build community.

Mutual aid is deeply reparative for our oppression-based stress and trauma. Every time we support someone else or feel supported through mutual aid, we experience a mismatch. We can fight for each other and show up to give each other what we need.

Healing Powers of Access Intimacy

Mutual aid isn't the only way to heal through community. When someone in our community, friend circle, or family understands our physical and emotional needs and meets them freely and lovingly, we experience what disability activist Mia Mingus calls access intimacy.[11] Access intimacy is any act that shows we know someone's needs and boundaries, and understand their feelings.

For some, access intimacy could be someone choosing a restaurant based on its accessibility for their friend's mobility device. It could be ensuring you have a chair that will be comfortable for your loved one's body. For others, access intimacy could be a friend making sure a gym class has childcare for your kid, that a group trip is within a price range that works for everyone. It could be remembering someone's trauma anniversary or giving a friend who survived sexual assault a trigger warning for a movie or book.

When we consider each other's needs and experiences, we fight against a world that feels like it is constantly not for us. We can show up for ourselves and our community through considering the needs and comfort of others.

Healing in Shared Spaces

Another way to heal through community is by literally *sharing space*—spending time with others who share our experiences and understand us. When this happens, our bodies relax. The masks drop. We don't have to be on guard or as vigilant.

I know what it is like to be healed in community. I didn't "become real" until a rowdy group of dykes, queers, and trans folks loved, danced, and fucked me into existence. For a solid ten years of my life after coming out, all I did was spend time with other queer folks. I see this in my clients as well. Once, a client told me, "I just want to be around other queer and trans people of color. Like, I want all my friends, lovers, the spaces I spend time in to be free of whiteness and heterosexuality." I get it. We all need and deserve spaces where we can be fully ourselves, totally authentic inside. Sometimes, those spaces have to be all we exist in for a while. They heal us. Make us real.

For those of us who are neurodiverse, disabled, chronically ill, or live rurally, online community is the space in which we experience feeling seen and have the freedom to express ourselves fully. My clients find community within support groups, online gaming, and community platforms like Discord servers. Here in St. Louis, a local dance studio named Yes Honey has started offering low-stimulation classes for neurodiverse folks. During these classes, the typically loud music is dialed down, the lights are low, and there is a space available at the back of the studio to get some alone time if people need it. The same studio hosts dance classes for new parents as well, which are baby friendly (you babywear and dance!) and have a nursing/bottle-feeding station and changing table.

Robin Wall Kimmerer writes in her book *Braiding Sweetgrass* about a weekly online group she attends to learn her violently erased ancestral language Potawatomi. Many Indigenous languages are extinct due to colonization—specifically due to Indigenous children being forcibly abducted from their family and sent to abusive boarding schools where they were beaten and starved if they spoke their native tongue. For Kimmerer, this language class is deeply healing for not only her but also her ancestral body, the connection we all hold to those who came before us. She is literally healing this generational wound through learning Potawatomi. Being in community with other Potawatomi people who share her trauma is a mismatch to our colonized society that separates Indigenous people from their community and culture.

Like-minded gathering spaces are not perfect. No place is. Most of us have also experienced more of the same in these spaces: trauma, rejection, feeling unseen and unheard. I have personally had my crotch grabbed forcefully, without my consent, by a man at a gay bar who said, "You don't have a dick—this bar isn't for you."

But I also know that a gay space is one of the only spaces that people in my community have to experience embodiment, art, and play. Finding a space where you fit means you can safely explore and celebrate your identity.

EXPERIENCING FREEDOM OF THE BODY

We must acknowledge that puritanical notions about sex and body modification have permeated and distorted the concept of morality in the dominant Western culture we live in. To liberate the body from these rigid notions is truly an act of resistance! For those of us who have been oppressed by society for the way we look or the way we love, for those of us who have been othered by our families or culture, for those of us who have suffered shame or rejection, experiencing freedom of the body is essential for radical self-liberation.

Healing Through Sex

Consensual sex is a reparative experience in a world that doesn't value your pleasure or your body. Feeling desired, having your pleasure prioritized, and being embodied during sex all serve as mismatches for many of my clients. Those who have suffered religious trauma and/or have deconstructed from their anti-sex religions find such a deep healing in their sexual freedom, though it can be a continued process of unlearning those harmful beliefs. My clients who live with chronic pain and illness and/or are disabled can experience sex as a way to be inside their bodies in ways that feel pleasurable. For sexual assault survivors, consensual sex can be a huge mismatch to their trauma, helping them heal their relationship to their sexuality and their bodies. Sex that is affirming for your body, gender, or sexuality, whatever it may be, is a healing practice.

In most parts of the world, especially since colonization, queer sex is seen as subversive, dirty, wrong, and evil. The queer community appreciates bondage, dominance, submission, and masochism (BDSM) because our sex is already demonized, so why not explore and accept all desires that are safe, sane, consensual? We queer and trans folks are much more likely to embrace explicit power dynamics during sex, play with the taboo, and explore fetishes than heterosexual people. Many people find BDSM to be a space of healing, self-expression, and embodiment.

BDSM invites us into our bodies because when you are playing with power and pain you have to be inside of your body. You must know your limits, your fantasies, what feels good, what feels bad, and for many people, what drives them to the edge of what they thought their bodies could do. BDSM is erotic, meaning it is of the body. It is intentional, and it creates a safe space to center one's body, desires, and creativity.

BDSM can be healing for survivors of sexual trauma because within that space, they get to choose what happens to them. Now they are in control, or it is their choice to give up control. With BDSM, all parts of us are welcome. The parts of us that have been labeled disgusting, blasphemous, and perverted are instead embraced, cherished, and celebrated. Taking what we've learned in chapter 4 on parts work, imagine how healing that can be for those parts that have always felt too much, too sexual, too perverse to get to engage in exactly the kind of sex and fantasies they desire. It is enormously healing to have another person, or many people, say, "This is a wonderful, acceptable, and beautiful thing about you."

BDSM can be a healing and transformative space for all folks at the margins. For folks with chronic pain and disability, BDSM can provide them with the place for their bodies to be cared for and explored in a nonmedical setting. For many people who have chronic illness and live with a disability, their body has become a medicalized object, something to be diagnosed, poked, or prodded. Our ableist society views people with disabilities as nonsexual humans. Here, in play, their bodies are sexual and celebrated. BDSM can allow for someone to reexperience their body as theirs, as a living, breathing being.

There are many people of color of all sexual orientations and genders in the BDSM world as well. In an article for *Salty*, nonbinary Black writer-activist B. Vanessa Coleman writes, "In a world where the Black body is relentlessly exploited, policed, and violated in ways that deny our autonomy and leave us perpetually navigating pain and trauma, kink+BDSM set us free by centering consent and encouraging self-expression and exploration, creativity and play. . . . In kink scenes then, Black folk can live free of the fear of experiencing any violence, harm or *anything* we didn't choose."[12]

BDSM offers a mismatch for oppressed bodies of all kinds.

The workshop of mine that is the highest in demand is called Healing the Nervous and Attachment Systems Through BDSM. I'll tell you why it's so popular: because we are only now in my queer community calling BDSM what it is—a radical embodiment practice. Nearly every somatic psychotherapy modality or creative embodied movement available to us has the central goal of getting out of our heads and into our bodies. These practices move energy through and out of the body, slow us down, and help us check in with our body's sensations and messages. I can think of no better safe space for this than BDSM.

When BDSM is safe, sane, and consensual, it allows us to release built-up stress hormones and energy in the body and to be fully known. Every part of us is welcome. We can have our wants and needs respected and listened to. We can have reparative experiences that mismatch what life is like day to day as marginalized people from any group. I will never forget the powerful scene I witnessed at a Kink Out event in New York City: two pro dommes, both femme, both women of color, using a single-tail whip on a white cisgender man (consensually, of course).

Sex doesn't have to be kinky for it to be transformative. For some queer people, having sex with other queers is the first time they have had a positive sexual experience. There is a particular trauma that some of us experience, sometimes for years, of having heterosexual sex that isn't abusive before we come out. I had sex that was loving and consensual with a heterosexual partner before coming out, and it left me feeling dissociated at best and disgusted and horrified at worst. Everything about it felt wrong, like self-abandonment. I couldn't understand why. My boyfriend loved me. He knew to ask and listen to my body's needs. He did everything from a place of respect. But it felt like a kind of death.

Most queer and trans folks have this experience, or much, much worse. Queer folks are four times more likely than heterosexual people to experience sexual abuse.[13] Almost half of trans and gender-diverse individuals will be sexually assaulted in their lifetimes.[14] So you can only imagine how profound it is to experience sex in a way that feels safe, consensual, and aligned with one's desires.

Or, on the other hand, for asexual people, it can be powerful to take sex off the table. Many people who are asexual either identify as queer in their romantic interests or feel like a part of the queer community because of their alternative sexual identity. People who are asexual tend to find sex uninteresting, upsetting, triggering, messy, or unnecessary for intimacy and connection. Just as queer sex can be healing for someone's body and their parts, deciding not to have sex with a partner who accepts and loves them as they are is just as healing. Not having sex and finding other ways to be close to a partner is just as radical, is just as embodied, as any liberatory sex might be.

The Freedom of Performance

Think back to your high school's theater performances. How many of the kids who shone under the lights of the auditorium singing their hearts out or belting out lines were quiet when they weren't onstage. A kind of liberation happens during a performance that doesn't happen anywhere else. Performance is where we can shed the everyday reality we are stuck with and embody another reality. And within this other world, we can be free of judgment, free of society's expectation, momentarily free of oppression. Within this ephemeral moment, worlds are destroyed and rebuilt. And the audience is part of that bubble of suspended disbelief. We're all in it together.

Whether it is onstage performing or as a participant of theater, a drag show, a concert, performance art, stand-up, improv, or any shared experience, we—audience and performers—all travel to the same place in our minds together. And it is profoundly transformative.

In his book *Cruising Utopia*, José Esteban Muñoz explores the drag-show stage as a portal that shows the crowd what a queer future, a queer utopia, could look like, a place of queer identity expression, embodiment, and celebration. During a performance, queer people can feel the possibility that this level of acceptance and celebration might last forever. To feel freedom in community with other queer and trans folks, other artists, other bodies like yours, is a corrective emotional experience. Outside is a world that constantly rejects our bodies. But here, performing onstage or dancing and singing along—and for those in drag, feeling hot in the look they've spent hours putting together—these experiences return us to our bodies. It's always disappointing when the lights come back on. The show is over. But we have glimpsed a reality that we can all cherish.

The stage is a site in which a culture, a craft, can be celebrated. Youngmi Mayer, a comedian, writer, and author of the memoir *I'm Laughing Because I'm Crying*, has made the comedy show (a space that is historically dominated by white cis straight males and one in which sexual abuse is rampant[15]) a community gathering place for Asian people, women, and biracial folks. During her shows she wears a hanbok—a traditional Korean outfit, which she likes to call "culturally appropriating my own culture."[16] She has her audience laughing until they cry. Nothing about her comedy shows is whitewashed for a white audience. She is making and performing comedy for other Asian Americans, for other immigrants, for other biracial people. Her comedy shows, in which she invites other Asian comedians to perform, are a by-us-for-us space.

Body Mod, Fashion, and Movement

Piercing, tattooing, and body modification have long been ways to express identity in cultures throughout the world. Today, they can be a way for marginalized people to reclaim their bodies in an oppressive world.

Tattoo artist Tamara Santibañez writes in their book *Tattooing as Liberation Work* that getting tattooed represents a type of ownership over one's body.[17] For anyone who has experienced oppression-based trauma because of their bodies, their identities, or their ability, publicly displaying ownership of our bodies can be a revolutionary act—we reclaim ourselves from the oppressive systems around us.

Clothing is another form of self-expression through the body. Many of my clients find bodily autonomy and gender expansiveness through the clothing they wear. Macy Eleni, author of the book *Second Chances: The Ultimate Guide to Thrifting, Sustainable Style, and Expressing Your Most Authentic Self*, has built her career and her platform around using secondhand clothing and thrifting to unleash her inner authentic self. Her interest in fashion has helped her heal from depression and a decades-long eating disorder. The thrift store was the first place she felt she could express her most true self instead of conforming to the standard that is packaged and sold at the local mall. Thrifting is both a hobby and an ethical choice.

How we dress is also a way to express our inner world and feelings outwardly. Here in my home of St. Louis, we have two plus-size fashion boutiques combined into one beautiful storefront called Ethical

Bodies and The Good-ish. They not only sell exclusively used clothing but host community events for people with abundant bodies. People who don't fit into "straight sizing," meaning sizes XS–XL, are underrepresented in the fashion world—from models and advertising to the availability of extended sizing. This can limit self-expression for anyone who falls outside the norm. Spaces like Ethical Bodies and The Good-ish allow people with larger bodies to find clothing that can actually express their inner selves, their creative styles.

Many of my clients have also found immense healing and transformation in connecting with their bodies through dance, bodybuilding, yoga, running, hiking, and other forms of movement. "Exercise" has been wielded against so many of us as a way to get our bodies to conform to a white, thin ideal. Reclaiming body movement as a way to be inside ourselves, feel calm and capable, and connect with our authentic self is a mismatch. There are body-positive, disability centered, and queer spaces and groups that focus on the rest of us—like Disabled Hikers, a West Coast–based group that meets for hikes on trails that are ADA accessible, and also reminds us that hiking is about being close to the outdoors and connecting with your body—whatever is accessible for you in your body or that moment. For many of my clients, getting strong at the gym or weight training alone at home has led them to feeling safer in the world as women, queer and trans folks, and people of color.

HEALING THROUGH COMPASSION FOR YOUR INTERNAL PARTS

When we turn inward with compassion for ourselves, specifically compassion toward our internal parts, we create a mismatch with how the world sees us and treats us and how we have internalized those beliefs.

My client Lindsey did not have a kind inner dialogue with herself. She had internalized her parents' voices and was governing her inner parts using their style of parenting: harsh and direct, with rigidly high standards and no room for emotion or error. This was a huge problem for Lindsey, as she is a deeply emotional person. She was communicating to her inner family of parts what had been told to her every day in her family of origin: "Get over it, move on, no time for feelings." Her family had operated this way out of survival. Emotions = falling apart. Not feeling = how we survive. This is a direct result of living in white supremacy.

When she left home, she received a similar message from the outside world. As a Black woman, her pain, physical and emotional, needed to be hidden, and even more than that, denied that it was even real. She had also internalized messages from her family and society about perfectionism. However hard white people worked, she had been taught (and literally told) she had to work twice as hard, as a Black woman, to get half the pay and recognition.

In one of our sessions, I asked Lindsey if she would speak to her ten-year-old niece, who also had big feelings and is already feeling the pressure of perfectionism, the way she speaks to herself.

She quickly responded, "Of course not! I would tell her that her feelings are real and valid, and her worth is not based on her performance at school."

"What if you started speaking to yourself the way you would speak to her?" I suggested.

This began Lindsey's discovery of her inner loving parent, the opposite of her inner critical parent. For Lindsey, her inner loving parent was her invitation to speak to herself and her parts with compassion. Lindsey envisioned her parts through the inner family approach, which helps us see that we all have an inner loving parent, an inner critical parent, an inner teen, and an inner child.

Learning to speak to her parts with compassion, something Lindsey had longed for in all her childhood and teen years, created a mismatch to the messages she received her whole life, helping her to change the dialogue inside herself when life was hard, when she had big feelings, and when she felt pressure to be perfect. It is through compassion toward ourselves and our inner parts that we can experience some of the greatest liberation of all.

YOUR TURN

Somatically Integrating Liberation Experiences

Let's take some time to review the liberation experiences you have experienced and integrate them into your body and internal family of parts.

Think of a time in your life when you have felt in community with others, seen and understood, and/or freedom and liberation in your body. This could be a community in person or online, an experience of mutual aid or access intimacy, a sexual experience, an art performance you attended or were part of, or a demonstration or action for a political cause.

Just like with Container and Safe Place, bring yourself into this moment. What do you feel in your body? What sensations do you notice, what body parts do you become aware of? Now I want you to invite any part of yourself that you feel needs to witness this experience. What rejected, wounded, or guarded parts of self need to see you in this memory? Invite them forward. Once they have emerged, take them on a tour of this liberatory moment for you. What do they think? What do they

> feel? Stay with this experience for as long as you need to and repeat it as often as you need for it to become an ingrained mismatch for you, your body, and your parts.

BRINGING IT ALL TOGETHER

We've looked at how oppression shows up in our nervous system and sense of self the same way that major trauma does. We've learned that long-term exposure to stress is traumatizing. Through liberation psychology, we've discovered that for therapy to be validating, useful, and effective for oppressed peoples, we need to acknowledge that oppression as a constant drain on our mental well-being. You yourself have experienced healing from oppression in ways you might not have even recognized.

We heal both inside and outside of the therapeutic space: through community with others, freedom in your body, and compassion for yourself and all your parts. We can create mismatches and undo the damage that oppression has done and continues to do. Remember, repetition is what creates new neural pathways. New neural pathways show your nervous system that you can come out of a fight-or-flight response. You can experience safety. It can be safe, and even celebrated, to be you.

CHAPTER 6

Healing from Childhood Trauma

The number one reason clients find their way into our work together is the impact of childhood experiences that still affect them today. In this chapter, we'll explore three types of childhood trauma that profoundly affect all of us on the margins specifically: attachment wounds, the trauma of growing up different, and religious trauma.

Being wildly adaptive creatures, we all developed defenses to survive our childhoods. But this comes at a cost. We develop defenses instead of the ability to self-regulate. As we learned in chapter 3, our earliest attachment experiences inform and shape our nervous system and our sense of self for life. But those foundations aren't set in stone.

I'm going to share with you how to work with your defenses to understand your overwhelming feelings and to heal the injured parts of yourself. As always, you'll find pathways for healing in those three core branches of community, freedom, and compassion. You'll even get a chance to reparent yourself, learning to self-regulate as an adult the way you wish you'd been given the opportunity to develop as a child.

Childhood trauma is a single or recurring traumatic event that completely overwhelms a child's nervous system, makes them fear for their lives, and threatens their emotional and physical safety. However, a childhood doesn't need to be highly traumatic to still impact us in our adulthood.

CHILDHOOD WOUNDING

Often people are criticized for "blaming the parents" for every issue later in their lives. I somewhat agree with that criticism—we are certainly responsible for our own healing. However, there are aspects of holding our caregivers accountable for their misattunements and even harm done that are necessary for healing. We cannot minimize what happens when kids don't get their emotional needs met.

Attachment wounds occur during our earliest years. They're caused by what is called "insufficient parental engagement."[1] These wounds show up in our adult lives and inhibit our capacity to self-regulate, meaning we have trouble processing and tolerating our internal sensations and emotions. They also show up in our ability to be interdependent rather than codependent[2]—to take up space, be present instead of dissociated, or feel entitled to having wants or needs. People—myself included—may find themselves in relationships that replicate these wounds.

My client Gene was raised in a home where she was not able to develop a core sense of self. As a little girl, she helped her mother care for her older brother, who was diagnosed with a devastating illness. Her first memories of life are of being four years old and changing his diaper. At an age when she needed soothing and comfort from a caregiver, she was expected to be a caregiver, not only to her brother but to her mother, who was anxious and stressed out, and whom Gene tried to keep happy—an impossible self-assigned task. Gene's mother was a first-generation American who herself had been raised by trauma survivors. She wanted a "better life" for her own children than she had herself. This showed up as relentlessly high expectations of her daughter, as though Gene had to reach a certain level of achievement to make up for her brother's challenges. The only activities she allowed Gene to engage in were those that would look good on a college application. Gene's father was an evangelical pastor who ran the house like a church. When Gene wasn't caring for her brother or trying to meet her mother's impossible standards, she was trying to stay out of range of her father's rage, abuse, and proselytizing. He controlled the way she dressed, would not let her cut her hair short, and confined her social circle to children of church members.

Gene couldn't know as a child that someday she would escape her suffocating family home, come out as a lesbian, shave her head, and be diagnosed with ADHD and dyslexia. All she knew then was that she was a failure as a student and as a daughter, and that her own needs and feelings had to be hidden at all costs. Gene wasn't taught self-regulation by her parents, so she learned to manage her overwhelming sadness, loneliness, and depression by binge eating alone in her room at night. She self-soothed through food since there was no comfort or care available to her elsewhere.

Now, I want to be clear: Every single person on this planet has an attachment wound of some sort. There is no such thing as a perfect parent. Even good enough parenting can sometimes be unattainable. Some of us have more attachment wounding than others, and so have more work and healing to do. Trauma may be the number one reason why people develop coping techniques like dissociation, but attachment wounding can impact adulthood in some of the same ways. Attachment wounds can come from:

- Having disengaged caregivers who meet our physical needs but are unable to provide comfort, soothing, and emotional care. They may be checked out and dissociated or overwhelmed. Like Sam's parents, who provided food, clothing, and a bed but were unable, due to their own issues of trauma and addiction, to provide any emotional caregiving.

- Having caregivers who are present but deny that anything is wrong or minimize your emotions with statements like "It's fine" or "You're fine" instead of providing comfort or validating emotions. Lindsey's parents were like this. While she knew she was loved, her childhood trauma of being sexually assaulted by a doctor was invalidated and dismissed.
- Having caregivers who commit what is called traumas of omission or inconsistent parenting. Instead of the trauma being something that actively happened, traumas of omission are caused by what *didn't* happen. These occur when children didn't get enough—nurturing, co-regulation, quality time spent connecting and playing with caregivers, and so on.[3] Jo, who you met in chapter 3, had to find comfort in the woods behind their house, because their parents were too checked out to provide any kind of nurturing—physical or emotional.
- Having caregivers who actively invalidate and shut down emotions through language like "Stop being a crybaby" or "Everything is fine" when it's not, or who totally shut down around big feelings. Vee, who you met earlier, was a child who couldn't conform to their father's idea of gender. They often were told that their emotional distress was invalid, that they better "Stop being such a baby."
- Having overwhelmed and stressed-out caregivers who don't have time or capacity to slow down and be present with us. Gene's mother was in this category—totally overwhelmed by her controlling husband, the care for her chronically ill son, and the impact of her own childhood trauma. She was not emotionally present for Gene in any mindful or nurturing way.

- Having our emotional needs and inner world ignored or shamed by a parent. Vee certainly suffered from a parent who shamed them, and worse, physically abused them for nonconformity. Gene, too, suffered shaming by her mother when she was unable to perform to her mother's academic expectations.

When we experience childhood trauma and attachment wounding, we learn to defend ourselves from our environment, to carry on with life even though we frequently feel scared, unsafe, unloved, or invalidated.

However, even for children who have consistent enough, good enough caregivers, there are other ways in which childhood experiences can be traumatic.

THE TRAUMA OF GROWING UP DIFFERENT: BODY-SHAMING, NEURODIVERGENCE, AND IDENTITY

At my grade school in St. Louis, there was a group of cool, skinny girls who did gymnastics. Their bodies defied gravity as they performed every day at recess for the entire playground. I did everything I could to fit in, but my body was different. It was bigger. It wasn't able to flip and contort on the bars the way theirs could. I was frequently singled out as the one to be excluded, made fun of, ganged up on. I didn't quite fit, and it wasn't just my body, though that was the most obvious target. These girls were normal, and I was weird. I understood this on some deep level.

Then, in fifth grade, a miracle happened. Two new girls transferred to my school from bigger cities. I recognized them instantly as fellow weird girls. What a relief! Madison and Michaela didn't give a shit about gymnastics. They cared about Good Charlotte, vintage clothes, and *The Rocky Horror Picture Show*. They saved me. I have been a proud weird girl ever since.

These friendships allowed me to experiment with identity in a way I never had before. If I wasn't so worried all the time about fitting in, I could really get to know myself—not just my interests but what kind of person I was, what kind of friendships I wanted, and what I wanted from my life. I was developing a core sense of self. It was in the safety of these friendships that I said for the very first time, "I like girls." They didn't judge me. While the gymnasts started calling me "fat dyke" rather than just "fat," I knew that, at least by two friends, I was loved and accepted. Later, in my teens, I would be pushed back into the closet, but for now, at the age of ten, I felt safe. I love the story of being saved by the weirdos, and wish that was the end of it. But the truth is I had to leave my public school for private middle school to evade the bullying. And that early bullying left a deep scar that I still carry today.

Bullying doesn't just come from other kids. Sometimes parents, school administrators, faculty, and school boards can be bullies, too, especially for kids who are wired differently.

Diagnosis of neurodivergence is complicated because they present themselves in such a broad variety of ways. Children socialized as boys are twice as likely to get diagnosed with ADHD, as the symptoms they tend to display are more stereotypical of the hyperactive type, which shows up as difficulty sitting still. In contrast, girls often suffer in silence with inattentive type, which tends to manifest in difficulty staying focused, remaining on task, and managing time.[4] These symptoms don't get noticed at the same rates as the fidgeting. And children socialized as girls tend to internalize that they can't get tasks done, becoming convinced that something is wrong with them, so they overcompensate and overcorrect in other ways. Black and brown boys often get the diagnosis of oppositional defiant disorder instead of ADHD (or cPTSD, for that matter), which can feel like a school-to-prison pipeline in and of itself. Instead of making school a safe and accessible place to learn, teachers and administrators tell these kids they are bad, even criminal, and need to be reprimanded instead of supported. Kids who have autism don't always display typical or severe symptoms. You guessed it: It's mostly girls and kids of color who get missed here again. They learn to mask who they are by suppressing natural tendencies of expression and copying other kids and adults around them instead of being authentic.[5]

While people with autism, ADHD, or dyslexia, for example, often get called out for being different, for relating differently, and falling behind in rigid school environments, it's also true that bullying can contribute to neurological changes and have physical consequences.[6] My chronic mental health issues like OCD, anxiety, and depression began in grade school, while I was being bullied, and I know countless others who mark the start of a long battle with mental illness after the onset of peer rejection.

Trauma psychologist Arielle Schwartz writes in *The Complex PTSD Workbook*: "Children who are abused are at greater risk for the development of learning disabilities because of the impact of chronic stress and trauma on their developing brains. Additionally, children who have a learning disability or ADHD are at greater risk of being abused when parents misunderstand or are triggered by their children's cognitive differences, distractibility, or impulsivity."[7] Not all kids with ADHD were or are abused. But we need to begin to see the connections between trauma and neurodivergence—from the way trauma impacts the brain to the way being neurodiverse can lead to further rejection and harm from society, parents, and systems.

Neurodiverse kids are at greater risk of being not only misunderstood but also bullied.[8] And sometimes the bullying happens not at school but in the home. Neurotypical caregivers may be baffled and frustrated by their neurodiverse children. Neurodiverse caregivers may not understand their children's needs. Either can result in attachment wounding or even abuse.

Bullying doesn't just profoundly impact our social relationships and identity formation, it can literally be lethal for queer and trans youth as well as kids who are immigrants, aren't white, or anyone who doesn't fit the "norm."

I don't know a single queer or trans person who wasn't bullied by peers, family, or caregivers. Queer and trans youth have been murdered for being who they are or have felt so hopeless that they have killed themselves because they saw no other way. Many of my clients and loved ones who are trans feel an unspeakable grief in knowing they will never experience a girlhood, boyhood, or ungendered childhood that reflects who they are and instead were forced to grow up in a gender that wasn't theirs.

This brings us to our discussion of religion, a source of spirituality and beauty at its best and divisiveness and brutality at its worst.

RELIGIOUS TRAUMA

It's estimated that around one-third of all adults in the US have experienced religious trauma.[9] Not all religions or groups are abusive; there are many churches, synagogues, mosques, temples, and spiritual groups that work extremely hard to undo the legacies of abuse within religious and spiritual spaces. But some religious organizations have inflicted a lifetime of harm on those of us on the margins. The trauma we're about to explore also pertains to growing up in cults or totalitarian groups that exert control over members' minds, sense of self, and access to the rest of the world.[10]

Unfortunately, religious trauma tends to begin during childhood. This makes healing from it that much harder, since it occurs during the years of our lives when our brain, nervous system, and sense of self are forming. For most of my clients, the fundamentalist Christian churches of their childhoods left severe developmental impacts on them. Such impacts on children often go unacknowledged.

Marlene Winell,[11] a psychologist and educator specializing in religious trauma, coined the term religious trauma syndrome (RTS). She found that survivors of religious trauma have significant difficulties in the following areas:

- Difficulty with decision-making and poor critical thinking ability, black-and-white thinking. When information is limited and controlled, dysfunctional beliefs taught, and independent thinking condemned, it's impossible for children to develop critical cognitive skills.
- Negative beliefs about self-ability and self-worth. When normal human feelings are condemned, the result is profound self-doubt. This can lead to emotional issues including depression, anxiety, anger, grief, loneliness, difficulty with pleasure, and loss of meaning.
- Perfectionism, which as we know is a defense—that manager part stepping in to help us survive.

Even moral development can be arrested in tightly controlled environments where leaders or a rigid concept of God is the first and last word on morality. Members of these communities, especially children, don't ever learn to trust their own instincts or see themselves as a reliable source of judgment.

Physical abuse and physical punishment are also standard methods to exert discipline and control in organizations that adhere to strict patriarchal power over women and children. In any religious environment that uses abusive tactics, children grow up believing that human desires and impulses must be suppressed and therefore there is something inherently wrong with them personally. In any other context, we would clearly label this as childhood trauma. Growing up being told you are bad and that something is wrong with you is somehow only acceptable within the context of religion.

If we were born into or came of age within one of these environments, a true sense of self may never develop. It is confusing, painful, and time-consuming to develop a sense of self as an adult. I see this with anyone who survived childhood trauma, as they try to get these foundational years back but never fully can, and then have to grieve that loss itself.

Being active members of religious organizations requires time and resources, sometimes at the expense of the children who aren't getting their parents' full attention. Kids instead turn to the church or spiritual group for attachment. This is what makes it so difficult to leave. The hardest part is losing that sense of certainty that they are loved by God and/or by their community.

And leaving a religion leads to its own set of traumas, including loss of social networks, family ruptures, social awkwardness, and sexual difficulty from years of authoritative views on sex and sometimes physical sexual abuse. If you're unfamiliar with the secular world, it is totally disorienting to be thrust out into it. After leaving a cult, people can feel like a fish out of water in the outside world. They have relied on leaders to be the arbiters of truth and as a result may have information gaps, especially for those educated in private schools affiliated with fundamentalist religions. Imagine if you had never been introduced to the concept of evolution, modern art, music, and on and on.

This damage is exponential if that person is also queer and/or trans. I have found that for queer and trans folks, specifically in the southern Midwest, religious trauma makes up the majority of their trauma experiences. Most of my clients grew up Southern Baptist, evangelical, Mormon, Christian Scientist, or Seventh-day Adventist. Extremist religions—spiritual and religious cults of any nature, rooted in Christianity or not—produce the same trauma responses and issues in life.

All of my clients with religious trauma also hold the trauma of familial/parental abandonment and rejection. For many of them, this is because their family of origin's religion sees them as bad, wrong, an abomination. Many LGBTQ+ youth are unhoused or experience homelessness in their lifetime for this exact reason—they are kicked out of their homes for being queer and/or trans. Many of my clients put off coming out for this reason; accepting their queerness and/or transness meant accepting their caregivers would kick them out, reject them. I have clients who come to our work literally not knowing who they are or even feeling real or human because of religious trauma.

As with all childhood trauma, religious trauma leaves us with a pile of discarded needs, a crushing burden of roles we think we have to fulfill to be loved, and a full arsenal of defenses.

DISCOVERING YOUR DEFENSES

Our defenses, in the language of Internal Family Systems work, are our protector parts, which we learned about in chapter 4. No matter the type of trauma or wounding we experience, we all depend on defenses to protect ourselves from overwhelming emotions and pain.

Defenses can be challenging to overcome in your healing process. Carlos, who experienced a traumatic immigration to the US as a child, is a perfect example. When we began our EMDR sessions, he had no emotions attached to his parental separation immigration trauma. He basically felt nothing. It was as if the immigration trauma—being separated from his parents—had happened to someone else. Carlos's defense was dissociation.

Dissociation is a common defense among people with childhood trauma or woundings. But there are many others that keep the trauma responses at bay so we can function in our day-to-day lives. Which of the following are all too familiar to you? Some common defenses are:

- Avoidance: "I just don't think about those things!" "I don't think or like to talk about my childhood."
- Addiction: "I drink, use drugs, overwork so that I don't have to sit with my emotions."
- Idealization: "I had a perfect childhood!"
- Need for control: "If I can control myself and other people, everything will be fine." "I'm not a perfectionist, you're just doing it wrong!"
- Dissociation: "I don't feel anything about my childhood." "I don't have any memories of my childhood."
- Denial: "It wasn't that bad." "Other kids had it worse." "I probably wasn't sexually abused; I must be misremembering."
- Denial of anger specifically: "I don't really feel anger." "I know I should be angry at my uncle, but I'm just not!"
- Narcissism: "I'm not the problem, everyone else is." "My way is the best way." (This often occurs when a child was raised believing they are worthless and have needed to overcompensate through narcissism to develop the self-worth they should have gotten through loving, attuned caregivers.)

Often, our defenses have been protecting us for so long from feeling overwhelmed by memories that we can't tap into the grief, fear, and sadness associated with them. Sound familiar? Defenses (or our protector parts, like our managers and firefighters) developed to keep the traumatized or wounded parts of us locked away so we can function. The legacy of childhood trauma is just that—we develop defenses and protectors instead of a core sense of self, an identity, and a regulated nervous system.

Remember that our defenses are there to keep us safe. We can't judge them, but we can get to know them. Here's an exercise to help you get to know yours.

YOUR TURN

Part 1: Defenses and the Body

Let's use our body to understand how defenses keep us safe. Pick a small object in the space you are in that will represent any responses or overwhelming feelings you experienced due to traumatic childhood experiences or attachment wounds. Imagine this object holds all of your repressed emotions and impulses from childhood. How do you feel toward this object now that you have stored all of those big, overwhelming feelings, painful memories, and fears inside of it? Is it hard to look at? Do you feel yourself wanting to move away from it?

Now choose a second object that can obstruct your view of the first object you've stored all those big feelings in. This could be a bigger object, a piece of paper, or even a wall. Anything that makes it impossible for you to view the original trauma object. How do you feel in your body now that you don't have to look at the trauma object? What do you notice?

This blocking object symbolizes your defense or your set of defenses. It's drinking, drugs, dissociating, self-harm, overworking, overeating, undereating, overspending, perfectionism, and so on. It allows you not to have to look at or experience the impact of those traumas on you. It allows you to lead a somewhat normal life. As a child, you were able to go to school. As an adult, you hold down a job. What are your defenses?

Part 2: Banishing Needs

Now select three new objects from the space you're in, things you can easily move around—for example, a pen, rock, and water bottle. Bring all of these items close to you. When you were a child, you had physical, developmental, and emotional needs, as all children do. These objects represent normal, reasonable needs you had as a child. The first represents all your physical needs: safety, a home, clean clothes, food, transportation to school on time (as well as to doctor's appointments and other activities). The second represents an emotional need of yours, like validation of emotions, your caregiver slowing down when you are sad, overwhelmed, scared, or disappointed, and saying, "I'm sorry you're feeling sad. It's so hard to feel that way. I'm right here." The third object represents a developmental need you had, whether it was for play, exploration, learning, or identity formation.

Now, let's say that you had a caregiver who wasn't able to regularly meet these needs, whether that was because of lack of access to resources, mental illness, or a parenting style that wasn't nurturing or compassionate.

Take your first object, those physical needs that a child has, and push it away from your body. As a child, you had a lot of physical needs that went ignored or weren't met. Maybe you didn't have a safe home, clean clothes, or enough food. Maybe you had to fend for yourself or your caregiver was never on time dropping you off at school or picking you up. As an adaptive little kid, you learned to just not have those needs. You learned to dissociate from your body because it's been made clear that your physical needs can't be met. The first object you've pushed away from your body represents a fragmented part, a part that holds your physical needs. You wisely expelled it from your body to get through your childhood. It hurt too much to look at this part, so you used a defense to not look at it. You banished this part and its needs.

Now take the second object and push it away from your body. These are your emotional needs. Maybe your caregiver didn't have time to slow down and be with your feelings because they were forced to work long hours to make ends meet. Maybe they themselves were raised in a family where children were seen and not heard, and they raised you the same way. Maybe you actually had to be the parent to your caregiver and you can't access your emotional needs because your caregiver hijacked the relationship and made you the parent. Well, now you have another fragmented part. A part of you that holds all of your emotional needs, your big, overwhelming feelings, your need to be comforted and cared for. This part also lives outside of your body now so that you don't have to sit with the overwhelming pain of not having these needs met. In order to not feel the pain and grief this part holds, you have to dissociate yourself from this part of you that has emotional needs. Later in life, when you are trying to build authentic relationships, you find yourself either in relationships where there is still no space for your needs, leading you to those questions like "Why do I keep dating the same people over and over who can't give me what I want?" Or you find yourself in a safe relationship, where you *can* have emotional needs, but when asked what they are, you draw a blank. Maybe you find yourself in relationships where you become the emotional caretaker of your partner.

Now push the third object away from you. These are your developmental needs, like the time, space, and safety to explore and play freely. Maybe you needed to work at your parents' business since you were a child. Maybe you never felt like you could explore and play because home wasn't safe or you had to grow up too fast. Well, just like those other parts of self, that need for developmental exploration and creating an identity separate from our caregivers gets fragmented and lives outside your body, with defenses to keep you away from the overwhelming grief and sadness that those needs can't be met.

Part 3: The Wound of Caregiving the Caregiver

As children, we might take on the role of caregiver for our parents to keep peace in the family. We do this because whatever happens at home gets normalized, so we may literally think it is the job of the child to support our caregivers. When our caregivers expect us to take on the caregiving role, we push our needs away, fragment from them like the objects you have pushed away from your body, and we become the child they need us to be instead of a healthy child with healthy needs.

Find a few more objects around the room that you can use to label roles you had to take on to keep your caregiver happy, to meet *their* needs. You had to give up your three objects and push them away, and instead have taken on these new objects, these adult roles, for your caregiver. Maybe you took care of their physical needs—cleaning the house, cooking the food, making sure you and your siblings got to school on time. Or you became the caregiver for their emotional needs—providing comfort or being the dumping grounds for their feelings and complaints. Many of us learned to check the vibe of our caregiver when they got home. What role did they need us to take on when they walked in the front door? Did they come in angry and need us to be the invisible child? Did they come in sobbing and need us to be their therapist? Did they come in overwhelmed by all their tasks and need us to jump into caregiver mode? See how crowded your space is with these rejected parts and adult roles you took on? This is how structural dissociation can happen—we have so many parts of self that we lose any coherent sense of self and never get to develop a core identity.

HOW WE HEAL: IDENTITY FORMATION AND SAFE RELATIONSHIPS

So how do we learn who we really are? How do we heal from this separation from our self? We heal both through our own solo exploration and through safe relationships.

When Gene went to college at age eighteen, she began the slow process of identity formation.

Finally away from the control of her parents, she came out as queer, got tattoos, and shaved her head. She learned to set boundaries with her mother and became estranged from her father. However, she spent the next decade of her life still trapped by the lessons she had learned in childhood, by the neural pathways that had been laid and strengthened as her role as caregiver, people pleaser, and the "easy" child.

As an adult, Gene found herself in relationship after relationship with chaotic, critical, and cruel people. Gene struggled with classic codependency. She was so focused on what other people needed, what other people wanted her to be, that when we began our work, she had no idea what she wanted for herself. Gene had fragmented the parts of her that had needs, interests, and big feelings as a very young child. Calling those parts back to herself was going to take a lot of time and hard work.

In her early thirties, Gene found herself in the first partnership in which she didn't have to manage the other person's rage and moods or abandon her true self to get love. Interestingly, she met Crystal because they were *both* seeking help in Co-Dependents Anonymous (CoDA). Gene and Crystal were both the kind of people who stayed high functioning, cut off from big emotions, and tended to attract chaotic people who needed a lot of emotional caretaking and managing. They both grew up in religious homes and were abused for being different: queer, neurodiverse, and unable to live up to their parents' impossible standards. As they saw what life could be—dating someone who didn't require them to become what the other person wanted and needed—Gene and Crystal experienced compassion for their selves, another core experience to heal your oppressed body, in their safe and loving relationship.

It dawned on Gene that this life she thought she couldn't have—one where she was free to explore herself and her interests and be spoken to with love and compassion at home—was actually possible. She didn't have to stay in the holding pattern of dating people who she needed to take care of or to ignore her core Self to get acceptance. It was this safe relationship that allowed her to finally ask in our sessions, "What do I want? What do I need? What do I feel?" As we excavated this belief system, it became clear: Gene had learned in childhood to ignore her own body's signals, focus on what other people needed, and mask her authentic, neurodiverse self.

For her, healing from childhood trauma has been allowing herself the freedom to explore "frivolous" interests like rock climbing and bootblacking,[12] activities that make her feel inside of her own body instead of cast out of it. Gene is learning who she really is through dedication to forming an identity apart from a caregiver and people pleaser, and being in a safe relationship that doesn't completely replicate her childhood, but instead is a total mismatch from it.

HEALING BY REPARENTING YOURSELF

In chapter 4, you learned about the transformative power of tending to and unburdening parts of Self that were created by trauma or attachment wounding. There is no better application of parts work or Internal Family Systems than reparenting yourself—in other words, giving your parts what you did not get in childhood.

In our sessions, Gene and I worked with the parts of her that she had fragmented herself from in order to endure her childhood. We invited these parts to show up and get to know the new Gene and this new life of hers, a process that is called updating. Gene realized that while she was able to enjoy her new world, her younger parts hadn't gotten the memo about what life was like now versus then, including the freedom she had and the compassion she experienced through her healthy and happy relationship with Crystal.

I invited Gene to choose a meeting place for her parts. She chose the climbing gym, as this was a space that was safe for her, and that she felt her younger parts would be in awe of. Gene and her inner parts sat around in a circle on the mat below the bouldering wall and built an inner community with each other. They did this through Gene hearing from each and every part about their experiences and what they thought about her, adult Gene. She listened with love and compassion, validating how hard it had been to have so many big feelings and nowhere to go with them. She did this with her inner child, who felt lonely, confused, and abandoned most days, and with her inner teen, who felt suffocated, ashamed, and not good enough. She even made space to hear from her inner critic: the part of her that had internalized the voice of her parents and society and constantly told her she wasn't good enough. These parts slowly began to trust Gene, her adult self who was now trying to become her own inner loving parent. The more her inner child and inner teen trusted Gene, the more her inner critic stepped back so Gene could speak to herself and her parts with kindness. Eventually, Gene was able to show her younger parts the big, expansive, authentic life she had built. She realized her younger parts still felt trapped in that apartment with her parents, taking care of them and her brother. She asked them if they wanted to come live with her in her life now, and they took her hand with an enthusiastic "Yes!"

We all heal through mismatches just like Gene did—through safe relationships that don't replicate childhood dynamics, that give us room to discover who we truly are. We heal through unmasking, allowing ourselves to express our body and mind freely, instead of conforming to a neurotypical, cisgender, white, or hetero standard. What this looks like is unique to every person. For Gene, it was freedom in her body to explore hobbies that were just for her, ones that got her into her body. It was a relationship with a partner who she—literally for the first time—doesn't have to take care of or become someone else for. This is what liberated her from her childhood patterns. Gene knows that it will be a lifelong journey to give herself what she never got in childhood: time to play and explore, the chance to feel safe and loved for who she truly is, and the freedom to be authentic. But it is a journey she feels excited about instead of burdened or overwhelmed by.

YOUR TURN

Reparenting Your Parts

Take a deep breath and notice what emotions and body sensations are present. Know that any feeling or physical experience you are having is a part of you looking to be seen and tended to. Invite any parts to join at a safe meeting place. Maybe you meet them in the Safe Place that you developed in chapter 1. If this is where you want to meet your parts, where in your Safe Place can you all sit and talk? Is it around a bonfire? Is it under a special tree? Or would it feel safer for your parts to meet somewhere more neutral like a conference room table, or maybe a cozy living room? Notice what setting is most appealing for your parts, for you. What sounds and smells do you want to perceive? Is it birdsong? Is it the smell of fresh brewed coffee?

Who do you notice joining you at the meeting spot? Maybe you have a clear image of different parts at different ages, or maybe they appear to you as exiles and managers like we learned about in the Driving the Bus exercise in chapter 4, all having different roles within your unique inner system. If no parts come to you, then invite emotions or physical sensations to the table. They are parts and are welcome too.

Now invite each part to share how they are feeling. Invite them to describe when and where they took on the role they have in your internal system. Invite them to share with you what they did not get as kids but need now. Notice how you feel toward these parts of you. Is it hard to look at them? Is it easy to see them with love in your heart? Share that love with them, and if it's difficult to have love for these parts, notice the part of you that has judgment or shame connected to these parts. Ask the judgmental parts to separate themselves from you, and honor these parts too.

Now look at the parts of you that did not get what they needed in childhood. Imagine giving them what they needed, whether it's the space to have big feelings, to play, or to experience physical safety. This is the reparenting process. If a part is really stuck in the past, I want you to visualize liberating this part from your own childhood. As I say to my clients, "Get them out of there!" Bring this part of you to the updated present, showing them whatever safety or love you have access to now. Show them that you are a safe adult who is here to hold space for their feelings and meet their needs.

Now that you have learned what these parts need, how can you incorporate reparenting into your life? How can you create actual time and space to give yourself what you did not get as a child? You are exactly the person they needed but did not get access to as a child.

BRINGING IT ALL TOGETHER

How is it that we heal from childhood trauma and wounding? Whether we hope to recover from caregiver failures, religious or cult abuse, or bullying, we heal in the same way. We heal through corrective emotional experiences, or mismatches, to childhood trauma. We heal when we feel fully loved and accepted for who we are—whether by ourselves, our partners, our community, or Earth. We heal when we are able to develop a core sense of self or be unburdened from the heaviness of childhood traumatic experiences. When we excavate our belief systems developed in childhood and build new ones, we heal.

CHAPTER 7

Healing from Legacy Burdens and Inherited Trauma

I always ask clients what they know about their lineage. Was there individual and collective trauma? Persecution? Addiction? Abuse? In most of my clients' ancestry, there is major trauma, ranging from war to colonization to the transatlantic slave trade. For many of them, it might also include generations of sexual abuse, domestic violence, alcoholism, or poverty. While ancestral trauma is never the sole reason for someone's trauma, it can be a major contributing factor, and it is the one that lives in the deepest part of us, at our core. In this chapter, we will explore how trauma experienced by our parents, grandparents, great-grandparents, and beyond still lives on in our own minds and bodies. We'll take a look at what happens to us, even generations later, on both a behavioral and a cellular level. This may sound like we are bound to feel the profound impacts of our ancestral trauma forever, but there are ways to help us let go of these burdens. We don't need to carry them forever. We can heal through compassion for our ancestors and their traumas; through the freedom that comes with fully living our identities and letting go of inherited burdens, beliefs, and behaviors that have kept us stuck; and through community with our wounded inner parts. I'll help you create mismatches to learn new ways you can liberate yourself from generations of trauma. You can honor your ancestors' experiences while still creating new, safer ones for yourself.

MY OWN ANCESTORS' TRAUMA

My ancestors lived through years of persecution because of their religion, ethnic group, and political beliefs. Their story, and the story of their descendants, illustrates how trauma trickles down through generations—impacting mental and physical health for over a hundred years.

In 1920 my maternal great-grandfather fled for his life, escaping from Russia because he was both a Jew and a Socialist, escaping on foot and making the journey from Moscow to France to find a ship where he could stow away. During the pogroms, my great-grandmother was buried alive and given a straw to breathe through by sympathetic Christians who hid her on her escape from Russia. They each sailed to America, where they were turned away at Ellis Island because the US had met their "Jewish quota." They both ended up in Havana, Cuba, where they met and raised two children—a daughter and a son.

When he was twenty-five, their son, my grandfather, traded his service in the Korean War for US citizenship. He and his parents and sister came to the US, to St. Louis, Missouri, not only as Jews but as Spanish-speaking immigrants.

I am the third generation in my maternal lineage to not live with the day-to-day threat of violence and murder. However, throughout stressful periods of my life, I have experienced debilitating obsessive-compulsive disorder (OCD). The terror, fear, and obsession with safety, despite my mostly safe environment, could be explained by the trauma living inside me and in my upbringing, inherited from my parents through their parents, and their parents before them.

Each generation's trauma also impacted their ability to attune to their children. Imagine traumatized caregivers overwhelmed by fear and obsessed with safety. They transmit their anxiety to their children through hypervigilance and overprotectiveness or strict control.

Childhood development is influenced by nature, nurture, *and* by a third factor: the experiences of our ancestors. Trauma is literally passed on to children over the generations, chemically influencing our genes. Epigenetics is the study of how certain genes are turned "on" or "off" due to life experiences and trauma. My great-grandfather who escaped Russia died from cancer. My great-grandmother who was buried alive to save her life developed schizophrenia. Their daughter, my great-aunt, had been a famous piano child prodigy in Havana but rarely played once she emigrated to the US. She struggled with drinking and drug use and died by suicide. Were their illnesses related to their early trauma and the trauma in their genes?

THE SCIENCE OF EPIGENETICS

Trauma impacts us generationally in nuanced ways. It impacts the kind of caregiving we get, the environment we grow up in, and our connection with our identity. It can even impact our DNA.

The field of epigenetics has shown how early stressful experiences alter our biology. When we're embryos, our gene expression is impacted by the person who carries us in their womb getting the proper nutrition. We can also be negatively impacted by our birth parent's consumption of alcohol, drugs, and events that flood them with stress hormones. Stress and trauma don't actually change the genes we carry, but they can determine the way our genes get expressed.

Here's where things get interesting. We don't just inherit genes. Throughout our lives, we're also affected by the gene expression that we inherit. When gene expression is modified by environmental factors, it can be passed to the next generation.

Gene expression can be altered by methylation, a process in which a chemical signal is added to a gene to activate or deactivate it. This alteration in function leaves a marker that can be passed on to the next generation. These changes can be both inherited and impacted by a person's lived experience.

Rachel Yehuda, professor of psychiatry and neuroscience and the director of traumatic stress studies at Icahn School of Medicine at Mount Sinai, studied the intergenerational transmission of trauma effects in the children of Holocaust survivors,[1] but her findings are meaningful for all traumatized offspring from people who come from a lineage of colonization, slavery, and displacement of First Nations and Native American communities, people who endure genocide, ethnic cleansing, or war—extreme traumas that live on in generation after generation. Yehuda found that in children of survivors, there was a change in gene methylation, which can change someone's likelihood of developing physical and mental health problems and diseases. So while it's still incorrect to say that trauma *directly* changes someone's genetic makeup, it can impact the process of gene expression and alter genes through methylation.

One theory of epigenetics is that changes in DNA from methylation are evolutionarily advantageous to the offspring of survivors should the stressor/trauma occur again or continue into the next generation. In a study on roundworms, researchers found that after being exposed to or ingesting a harmful bacteria, the worms passed on an avoidance of that bacteria to their offspring.[2]

With worms, traumatic stress and danger responses can be passed on for four generations. Research shows that the genetic legacy of trauma can be felt through *at least* three generations.[3]

How our ancestors' trauma impacts us physically happens on a microscopic level. It's easier to see how such trauma impacts us behaviorally. Most children mirror the behaviors and beliefs of their parents. If that behavior is influenced by trauma, that means the next generation lives as if they experienced the trauma firsthand.[4] This is called inherited PTSD.

WHEN THE LEGACY OF GENERATIONAL TRAUMA IS PTSD

My client Mariam is someone who holds generations of trauma in their body. As a queer, nonbinary Lebanese American living today, they also experience racism, Islamophobia, misogyny, and more on a regular basis. Their parents escaped the Lebanese Civil War and immigrated to the US, then experienced profound xenophobia and Islamophobia, especially after 9/11. Many of Mariam's family members who also survived the war have serious physical illnesses and loads of vicarious and firsthand traumas they have never been able to process. Their family just doesn't talk about those "bad times."

Mariam is someone who has a historical trauma response, or an HTR[5] (which is also referred to some in people's lineages as a colonial trauma response, or CTR).[6] These terms can be applied to our lives if our ancestors experienced trauma as a result of historical events like genocide, colonization, or enslavement, and all the ways their violent legacies continue throughout generations.

Those of us with an HTR or CTR experience both the intergenerational trauma burden and its cumulative buildup over generations. Sometimes that's multiple generations of traumatized caregivers. On top of that, we experience our own traumas in our lifetimes like oppression, discrimination, lack of access to lifesaving resources, microaggressions, and loss of identity, just to name a few.

What does this kind of generational trauma look like in us? Some examples of the responses are:

- Feeling numb
- Dissociation
- Hypervigilance
- Nervous system dysregulation
- Psychosomatic symptoms
- Intrusive images[7]

Sound familiar? These are also classic PTSD symptoms! Adaptations to trauma, including PTSD symptoms, are our bodies' ways of keeping us and our offspring safe in this world.

Yehuda was surprised to find that the children of Holocaust survivors had worse PTSD symptoms than their parents.[8] But why would children of trauma survivors have more severe PTSD symptoms than the person who actually experienced the trauma? Yehuda set out to discover how trauma gets passed on generationally. Studies have shown that children of Holocaust survivors and Vietnam War veterans have biological similarities to their parents and to other people with PTSD, specifically lower levels of the stress hormone cortisol.

People usually think of low cortisol as a positive thing, meaning you're not stressed out. But actually, not *enough* cortisol in the body can be a PTSD marker. (So is having too much.) Low cortisol is responsible for the parasympathetic activation of the nervous system during trauma causing avoidance, dissociation, fawning, freezing, and depression. Low cortisol is also one of the main ways people survive long-term traumas. The body makes less of the stress hormone so the trauma becomes less overwhelming. This causes people to numb out. Low cortisol has many negative physical and mental health impacts. We need a balanced amount of cortisol to feel healthy—not too much (which can cause overwhelm and anxiety) but also not too little (which can cause dissociation and depression).

For some of us, the trauma responses that result in too little or too much cortisol live on in our bodies, even when these responses are no longer linked to actual danger but are outdated information encoded in our genes. These trauma responses can be unlearned and let go of through acknowledging our personal safety and letting go of our trauma responses.

But for those of us on the margins who currently live with unsafety in the world for many of the same reasons our ancestors were unsafe, our work is different. That work is to acknowledge where our bodies still experience oppression and unsafety, but also to learn to ground in the "safe enough" present. We can hold on to the resilience our ancestors gave us and use that to survive in today's world, but also notice where we might be holding on to generational trauma responses that we don't need anymore.

HEALING INTERGENERATIONAL TRAUMA

So how do we heal intergenerational trauma? We have to first notice the ways our intergenerational trauma is impacting us, which tend to manifest with the following symptoms:

- Physical illnesses
- Using substances or engaging in other addictive behaviors to manage overwhelm
- Overworking—feeling like you can't rest or take time off
- Unhealthy or even abusive relationships

- Suppressing emotions
- Shame around sex or sexual identity
- Disconnection from your body
- Neglect of bodily needs
- Fear of loss
- Unprocessed grief of loss (of family members, land, culture)
- Actual lack of resources like food and money
- Fear of scarcity around food or money

What are some patterns in your life that you feel were passed down from your parents, grandparents, and ancestors? What physical illnesses do people in your family tend to have, especially ones that are associated with higher stress? Once you have identified your big generational trauma legacies, let's look at how we can start to heal them.

Epigenetics shows that our lives are not completely determined by our genes, and that our environment, and more specifically how we perceive our environment, has a huge impact on our gene expression. We are deeply impacted by the world around us, and while we had little control over our childhood years and many of us still live at the mercy of oppressive systems, there are aspects of our environment that we *do* have control over. We have control over how we treat our bodies, who we spend time with, what we do in our free time, the values we hold, the boundaries we set. This control can help us break cycles of past generations and help our bodies feel safer in the here and now, which has a tremendous impact on us, even on a cellular level.

BREAKING THE CYCLE

Cycle breaking[9] refers to the process of changing generational patterns in our lifetime so that they don't get passed on to the next generation. While trauma lives on in our lineages for generations in our genes, what can be changed now is our body's current environment and how we raise the next generation.

Specifically, what do we actually have control over? This is where I return to the core tenets of trauma healing for all of us: creating mismatches to our trauma or our ancestors' trauma through compassion, community, and freedom. These tenets can be applied whether or not you're still experiencing traumas your ancestors experienced.

The culture that Mariam grew up with was one of survival, at any cost to the body and spirit. They were raised in a family that didn't talk about feelings and frequently pretended that major issues just weren't happening. This was how their parents, grandparents, and ancestors had survived before them. There was a culture of "Don't slow down to grieve or feel, just keep going." When Mariam's grandmother died, everyone got one time to cry, and then were instructed to "be strong" and carry on. They learned to abandon their core Self—a queer nerd who loved fantasy novels and cosplay—and to assimilate and be as "normal" as possible.

As an adult, Mariam still tried to present as what they knew their family considered "normal." But it was painful to Mariam that they couldn't show their family who they really were. Mariam resented them. But when Mariam recognized that these family patterns—suppressing feelings and denial of self—were born out of trauma and survival, they felt a swell of compassion toward their parents, grandparents, and ancestors. Mariam was able to see the family's strict rules and lack of emotional capacity as a trauma response, one that had quite literally kept them alive. This response, Mariam realized, was the family's instinctive way to keep their child safe too.

Compassion has also allowed Mariam to break the cycle of ignoring their emotions, ignoring their body. That compassion meant slowing down and listening to their heart and body when emotional and physical pain arises. Compassion has meant learning to say "I am sad" or "I am tired" instead of suppressing and just pressing on. When they feel burnt-out at work, which usually manifests as a migraine or a skin rash, they take time off. They are working on unlearning the scarcity mentality they were raised with and personally needed to get through their early twenties.

Mariam created a community of other queer SWANA (Southwest Asian and North African) and BIPOC folks who have special interests like theirs, and they find comfort lamenting to each other about how their families see them as different and weird. In their community now, Mariam feels they can be their full queerdo self. They have even incorporated their family's lineage into their cosplay, building more community with their ancestors by writing a fantasy story about a queer ancestor who came to them in a dream.

Most important, Mariam has a sense of freedom in their life. They are free in their self-expression, their sexual identity, how they spend their time, who they choose to be around. Even though they still experience oppression, they are able to see how the inherited gifts of survival and resilience have led them to being able to break cycles in their lifetime that their ancestors were not able to by living authentically and having time for their own interests. Mariam isn't sure if their life will lead to parenthood, but they are close with their nieces and nephews and model for them a different way of living than the rest of their family.

Mariam's story shows that while we can't control our ancestors' experiences, how we were raised, or our environment as children, we can control our lives in our teenage and adult years. They broke the cycle. Think about that lowered cortisol Yehuda found in her studies on Holocaust survivors' children, who were living out the trauma responses of their parents. For those offspring, for Mariam, and for any of us with inherited trauma, living a life where we can feel safe(r) and free is a mismatch to what our bodies have experienced.

Mariam did actually need a lot of the survival responses that lived on in her body as an Arab person in America. But the environment they created for themselves was one where they were able to feel safe and connected to others. It isn't safe for them all of the time. But it is "safe enough." (Remember your "safe enough" protocol from chapter 1?) It is possible to both acknowledge how living under patriarchal white supremacy and other oppressive systems has an impact on us and at the same time hold the safety and authenticity we can access despite those material realities.

The more authentic Mariam's life became, the more physically and emotionally well they felt. I'm not saying that living authentically solves all our mental and physical health issues. I'm saying that our genetic expression and our cortisol levels are directly impacted by our environment. Mariam came out to their deeply religious mother, who, despite her religion, loves and accepts Mariam's queerness. Their parents don't understand or get their pronouns right, but their girlfriend comes to family dinners and is ultimately welcomed by the family. This took a lot of time, but Mariam's personal work helped them be able to honor their family's and ancestors' survival and resilience and accept their parents' long process of adapting to the ways Mariam did not conform to the family norms. Our ancestors determine what genes we have and how likely it will be for those genes to be expressed. Our environment determines which genes actually get turned on. Our caregivers and environment determine how stressed out we are, and thus the stress hormones our body releases. But we have a say too.

While our ancestors' lives and experiences live on in our bodies, we have the power to live fully, opening ourselves to healing. This doesn't mean we leave their experiences behind. We will always carry them with us. In fact, we can think of them with compassion for all they suffered and for the burdens they carried for so long. But we can also honor them by living our best lives, by breaking cycles that no longer serve us.

How do we do that? Cycle breaking can look like the following:

- Living in our authenticity (our political beliefs, personal interests, authentic gender expression, authentic sexual expression). Mariam did this through coming out as queer and nonbinary and embracing their nerd interests that bring them joy.
- Finding purpose in our life (not just living to survive). Mariam sees their greatest purpose in life as modeling for the children in their family what is possible: living your truth, feeling your feelings, not pushing down emotions or bodily needs. Their ancestors couldn't have imagined the freedom Mariam has fully embraced today.
- Healthy relationships with friends, family, and lovers. Mariam has a big, beautiful community of people like them who can fully understand them, and of late, after a lot of hard conversations, that even includes their mother. Mariam's relationship with their family has grown more healthy, authentic, and stable.
- Caring for our bodies. When Mariam is sick, they care for their body instead of ignoring its signals and pushing through like their parents and ancestors needed to do in order to survive.
- Slowing down and resting. Let's never underestimate the power of resting. When Mariam slows down, they are honoring their ancestors, who were not free to rest when they were tired. And they recharge their own energy and reserves to live their life fully and bravely.
- Decluttering the home and letting go of objects that no longer serve

you. When we keep too much of the past in the form of stuff, it can be oppressive. Ask yourself whether an object makes you happy. If not, you're under no obligation to keep it. You'll appreciate the freedom of the space this creates. Mariam donated clothes that no longer affirmed their gender to the local Goodwill. It was hard to not hold on to them "just in case," but in releasing these items, Mariam felt more emboldened to dress in the masculine attire they prefer.
- Sobriety or thoughtful engagement with substances.

Remember in chapter 4, you learned about unburdening and befriending parts? Your legacy of trauma is also a part of you that protects you. Let's explore how you can release those tightly held burdens and set them free.

RELEASING LEGACY BURDENS

In Internal Family Systems therapy, generational trauma is referred to as legacy burdens.[10] Our parts carry these as if they are personal burdens or traumas we ourselves experienced. You learned about unburdening parts in chapter 4 and can now apply this process to generational trauma.

In IFS traditions of healing, there is no way to heal in the here and now without healing past generations alongside us. Some of the burdens we carry simply do not serve us—in fact, they get in the way of our own healing. We do not need to carry them forever. Many Indigenous healing traditions have always included healing from these legacy burdens or soul wounds of the past generations.

We can imagine these legacy burdens as handed down to us without our consent. Like we are carrying a heavy load we did not agree to take on. Releasing them includes identifying when a burden is from our ancestral lineage versus our own personal trauma. Or, when it is both, figuring out what is ours and what has been passed down. We can then work with our parts to release these burdens back to where they came from or send them somewhere else, helping our entire ancestral body release them.

One of my powerful legacy burdens is my relationship to my body size. Humanity has a long, brutal history of women's bodies being policed for size, sexuality, and how they occupy space. This is a burden that still applies to my life. The women in my family spent their entire lives trying to force their curvy bodies into becoming thin ones. In the Ashkenazi Jewish diaspora, as in many other cultures, there is an association with bigger bodies as belonging to the people of the "shtetl," peasants from small towns in Eastern Europe displaced due to pogroms and expulsions. Thin bodies are associated with a higher class, with Western European Jews who looked "less ethnic." This is also true of other cultures, involving skin color and body size, with darker skin and abundant bodies being associated with lower castes.

As my ancestors assimilated in the US, it was within their best interests to either pass as non-Jews or, if perceived as Jews, at least be perceived as upper-class, Western European ones. Essentially, a fat body was an immigrant body, an ethnic body. A thin body was the ideal American body. And even today, despite the body-positive movement, there is still enormous pressure in our celebrity-obsessed culture to be thin or be in the "right" kind of curvy body. I was born with the "wrong" kind of body. If I lived in a thin body, it is true that it would be easier for me to shop for clothes. I might be perceived as more professional or better educated or even of a higher class. People might be nicer to me, and I would receive better health care[11] (if I had a dollar for every time a doctor assumed a health issue I was having could be cured by weight loss, I would be a rich girl indeed). As a child,

I was bullied for being fat. As a teen, I starved myself in an attempt to fit in.

And so, if I am going to let go of the legacy burden of shaming my own body, I'll need to check in with that awkward girl and that unhappy teen and invite them to come forward. As I sit here now and check in with my parts, I notice my teenage self surface. She's my fifteen-year-old exile. This is the part of me that first took on the burden of forcing my curvy body to be thin. She is hungry and miserable. But she is thin due to restricting food and abusing stimulants. She is proud of her ability to endure this pain and discomfort, and she feels good about herself when people notice her weight loss. I now ask her if this burden to be thin is hers, and she says yes, in order to get love and acceptance, she needs to carry this burden. Then I ask her if she will come with me. She is open to the idea. We walk together side by side on a beach where I have a clear memory of being this age and hiding my body with a beach towel, horrified by the way the water made my surf shorts cling to my thighs. I remember feeling so disgusting, so embarrassed. We leave that beach, walk down the shore, and arrive at a cove. It's a gay topless beach, and the event that is in full swing is called Fat Femmes and Friends Beach Day.

My twenty-five-year-old self is among the topless femmes. I show my fifteen-year-old self this scene: a sprawling landscape of queer and trans folks of all body shapes, but mostly fat, in some combination of brightly colored bathing suits or naked lounging in the sun and swimming in the ocean. My twenty-five-year-old self is being a flirt, getting up from a blanket with my girlfriend at the time to tease the couple hosting the event. I show my teen self how confident I felt that day, how desired. But most important, I show her that I belong, not in spite of my body, but because of my body. Because I am queer, and femme, and fat, this beautiful party is for me. My fifteen-year-old self softens. I ask her how it feels to see this alternative reality, just ten years down the line for her. She tells me she had no idea this was possible. I ask her again whose burden it is to be thin—hers, or someone else's? She thinks for a moment and says, "Not mine." She tells me she wants to let this go. She wants the beach, the sun, the community, the compassion for herself, and the freedom of bodily expression.

"Where do you feel the burden in your body? The burden to be thin?" I ask her. "Here," she says, and points to her belly. "Ah, I see," I tell her. "You have always been told you are too much for having a big belly." She nods. I show her my memory of a lover leading me into her bedroom, looking deep into my eyes and asking if she can worship my belly. I show her my belly, swollen and rotund, carrying my beautiful child. I ask her, "Do you see all that your belly can do?" She nods. She is ready to release the burden. "Where should we release it to?" I ask her. She points to the ocean. We walk, hand and hand, into the water, up to our knees. I watch as she lets the beach towel concealing her body drop, watch as the waves take it away. "They came here so I could be free," she tells me. "I am the first generation who actually can be." And with that, she walks away from the water and joins the party on the beach.

YOUR TURN

Releasing a Legacy Burden

Take a second to check in with yourself. What legacy burden do you carry that you feel ready to release? What is not yours but that you still carry? How can releasing this burden allow you to live the life your ancestors fought so hard for you to have? What survival tactics did they have to use to stay alive that don't quite fit your reality? What do you want to keep with you that they passed on (a lineage of resistance, survival, perseverance), and what are you ready to release?

Invite the part that best embodies your carrying of this burden forward. Ask them if this burden is theirs, or if it is someone else's. You might invite the part to release the burden with you after showing them how it is no longer needed, like I did with my part. Or you can encourage the part to release the burden back to the person who first gave it to you, and even imagine that person handing it back to the ancestor who gave it to them, and so on. When we release legacy burdens, it allows us to live in our authenticity, something that our ancestors ultimately wanted for us.

BRINGING IT ALL TOGETHER

How do we heal from the legacy of trauma? We acknowledge the ways in which our parents, grandparents, great-grandparents, and further back in time had to struggle to survive. Although their trauma may have altered our own gene expression and we may experience greater trauma symptoms than the generation before us, we still have the ability to heal. We can break the cycle of inherited trauma. We can release our legacy burdens and create mismatches for the trauma experiences held in our genes and in our behaviors. We do this through our evergreen sources of healing: celebrating community by being true to our identity, exploring freedom of body expression, and holding compassion for our ancestors and for ourselves.

For some of us, our ancestors' trauma experiences are still shared by us today. For others, the conditions that our ancestors suffered are different from our own lived reality. Whether or not the burden your parts inherited from your ancestors still applies to your life, releasing it can free you to develop your own way of dealing with stress or trauma—without carrying what isn't yours.

CHAPTER 8

Healing from the Trauma of "Modern Living": Surviving Capitalism and Global Traumas

We wake up tired—tired from another night of bad sleep, being kept up late by work, or racing thoughts about climate change and genocide. We don't have time to make a nourishing breakfast or take a second to check in with ourselves before starting another day. Maybe we have to get family members and ourselves off to school and work, and often the needs of others come before ours.

We commute to our jobs during rush hour on loud, crowded public transit or in cars stuck in long lines of traffic. We work all day, experiencing stress and physical exhaustion that our workplace normalizes and encourages. Whether we labor with our bodies or with our brains, both parts of us feel depleted by the end of the day. For many of us, the work continues long into the night. Maybe we work overtime or have a night shift, or stay up late answering emails in the evening. And at home, cooking, cleaning, and caretaking are hard work. Those who work from home are often forced to blur the boundary between private and work life, taking calls and emails every hour of the day, seven days a week, with no real sense of rest. All the while, our screens call to us, promising easy distraction and entertainment to take us away from this cycle of constant work and overwhelm. When we finally put down our devices to sleep, we feel emptied out.

We live disconnected from nature and ourselves, in environments that leave us sick and depleted. People who live near airports, nuclear waste dumping sites, and factories suffer higher rates of asthma, cancer, and other illnesses. Environmental racism is rampant, with 70 percent of superfund sites within one mile of public housing.[1] Cancer Alley is a section of the Mississippi River known as a sacrifice zone where oil refineries are bunched together on purpose to keep them away from wealthier, whiter neighborhoods. These refineries are built right on top of parishes that are inhabited by majority people of color. Thirty to forty percent of fresh produce, meat, and dairy products end up in landfills, while many people struggle to have enough food to eat.

The way our world functions is not sustainable for human life. It disconnects us from one another and from ourselves, from what we need most to feel whole and human.

In this chapter, we'll acknowledge all the ways "modern living" itself is oppressive. And then, we'll take a deep breath, and I'll share ways to help you heal from the daily trauma of the demands and horrors of late-stage capitalism, pandemics, and genocides. Our tried-and-true core branches of healing are there for us. I'll show you how having self-compassion can lift the burden of capitalism. Together, we'll explore the freedom already available to you through rest and the natural world. And we'll celebrate the ways we can heal ourselves and our communities, making us stronger and healthier. Our collective healing is tied up in both our individual care and mutual care of ourselves and one another.

THE TRAUMA OF GLOBAL CLIMATE CHANGE, PANDEMICS, AND POLITICS

My client Kate and I often talk in our sessions about climate change and the dangers of another global pandemic. Kate wonders what a large-scale climate disaster or another mass disabling event could mean for someone who lives with chronic pain and disability. The fear that Kate brings up most often is what will happen to those who depend on the supply chain to get medication and other medical needs met during a global crisis. At the start of the COVID pandemic, we got a taste of what supply chain disruption can look like: empty shelves, waiting months for certain essential items like masks and even toilet paper. For some folks, this sparked a creative spell, sewing cloth masks and reevaluating what they considered truly essential. Distilleries made hand sanitizer. Local businesses stepped up and offered home deliveries. But for many people who rely on the supply chain for lifesaving medical equipment and medication, disruptions are absolutely terrifying. Kate said, "If I can't get my medications, I won't be okay. There is no living off the grid or living off the land option for me when coastal cities become unsafe. I need access to medications and machines and medical care in order to stay alive." Kate's body is riddled with adrenaline and cortisol most days. They live in fear of what this changing world will mean for them and for all chronically ill and disabled people.

For some of us, disaster has already struck and deeply impacted our lives: We've lost our homes to wildfires, our loved ones to systematic violence and neglect or a pandemic. We've witnessed a global shift to the right and the rise of fascism. We've watched the rich get richer and the poor get poorer.

All this makes up the trauma of "modern living."

I put "modern" in quotes because this word, *modern*, has been used to place some cultures (white, Western) at the top of a hierarchy, and relegated others (Indigenous folks and people of color) to the bottom, labeling them as "primitive." But *modern* doesn't mean smarter, better, faster—it means degradation, destruction, and death. Modernity is the reason we are in the place we are in, why we are looking down the barrel of the gun of climate collapse. The idea of modernity has misdirected us. "Look over here," modernity has said, "look at this shiny object!" while greed has driven our planet to the brink. Meanwhile, the Indigenous people of the world have been in the right relationship with this planet for thousands of years; they developed practices of living on this planet that nurtured her, instead of destroying her.[2] "Modern" is the opposite of "better."

The trauma of "modern living" causes our bodies to release stress hormones as we are exposed to the news, watching genocide in real time on our phones, the realities of labor in profit-over-people capitalism, and climate change. As we've learned, daily stress shows up in our bodies in the same ways that trauma does. In our society, people are forced to live within a system that is focused on production over quality of human life, which is extremely stressful. It's dysregulating for our bodies and fragmenting for our sense of self. It's why suicide rates and addiction are on the rise among many groups.[3]

This "modern-day living" is hurting—even killing—some of us.

VICARIOUS TRAUMA

We are all dealing with what we in the trauma field call trauma exposure, meaning ongoing exposure to experiences, information, images, and knowledge that changes the way we feel about ourselves and the world. War and unthinkable acts of violence have long existed in our society. But we have never had such immediate access to firsthand accounts, photos, videos, and even livestreams of these events as we do now. This is a two-part phenomenon. On the one hand, we are able to be informed about violence that has historically been hidden. This means that there can be more collective action in response: protests, mutual aid, critical thinking. Knowledge is power, and when injustice is made visible, more change and healing is possible. On the other hand, our brains and bodies are not physically or mentally equipped to process so much violent and overwhelming information all at once. It is simply too much for our ancient nervous systems, which are designed to keep us alive at all costs but not made to decipher between what is happening to us and what is actually happening to someone else.

Vicarious trauma (VT) is exactly that—trauma that happened to someone else, but that we become exposed to and absorb secondhand.[4] People who work in high-exposure jobs—such as nurses, first responders, care workers, ecologists, therapists, teachers, and activists—are exposed to high rates of trauma that leave a mark, even if they and their loved ones are not yet directly impacted by trauma. Even those of us who don't have high-exposure jobs are now exposed simply by being bombarded by the awareness of the death of our planet, or at least the extinction of the world as we know it. Such exposure is an ongoing trauma.

VT functions like this: We have mirror neurons that "try on" other people's experiences so we can empathize with them, try to understand them. Mirror neurons are activated both when we perform an action and when we see someone else perform that action. Mirror neurons are why when we smile at a baby, they smile back. Why when our best friend cries, we find tears falling down our own faces. This is part of how we relate to others. These neurons function as part of our attachment system. Studies have shown when participants are shown images of faces looking disgusted, their brains light up as if they're smelling something gross too. Other studies have shown that these neurons light up when a person witnesses or recounts a story about something painful happening to someone else.[5] Mirror neurons are how and why we experience empathy and build relationships.

These neurons are also why we feel so overwhelmed and full of despair when we are exposed to violence online. We need to know what is happening in the world so we can do our part to speak truth to power and try to change things. However, the question remains: How do we take care of our brains within this violent world? How do we know when we are no longer gathering necessary information and witnessing others' pain and have crossed into territory that is harming us?

Symptoms of VT (also called secondary PTSD) are as follows:

- Feelings of hopelessness
- Hypervigilance
- Negative view of other people and the world: "People are inherently evil" or "The world is a bad place"
- Nightmares
- Intrusive images
- Low energy and fatigue
- Existential distress
- Withdrawing from other people
- Increased alcohol and drug consumption
- Low appetite, or binging foods that make you feel sick
- Increased screen time

Many of these symptoms may look familiar to you. They mimic symptoms of PTSD. None of us is exempt from the feelings that stem from this exposure. And yet these collective traumas are finally being named as such. I rarely see the recognition in my field of psychotherapy that trauma is not just something that happens during childhood, a specific event later in life, or even those acts of aggression we specifically experience as oppressed bodies, but is actually part of our daily reality living in this world for *anyone* who is paying attention.

That attention becomes hypervigilance when we cannot escape witnessing the violence and suffering of others. And our nervous systems react as though our own bodies experience that trauma.[6] One way of viewing this is to acknowledge how, at our core, humans are deeply compassionate, and how interconnected this entire planet is, despite what capitalism wants you to believe.

CAPITALISM CUTS US OFF FROM SELF

Self, that essence of who we truly are at our core, is hard to connect to when we are in a survival response. When our protectors—those managers and firefighters—are activated, our Self-energy dims. We get stuck in protector mode. We can lose connection to who we truly are, what it is we really want from life. Trauma robs us of our ability to connect to Self. Childhood trauma means we don't get to build a solid foundation of Self. But so does capitalism.

Capitalism keeps us stuck in hustle mode. We are so busy working, trying to stay afloat, that we can't get quiet and drop into our bodies. If you have ever worked a fourteen-hour shift—serving, nursing, or in retail, then you know what I mean. You literally have to leave your body to get through. These jobs rely on our inherent caretaking abilities. Our role is to be mother, lover, caregiver to our clients or customers. These fields are incredibly gendered and incredibly exploitative. We live in manager mode and shift into firefighter parts when we clock out: dissociating, drinking, using drugs, buying shit, isolating, restricting, or binging.

Our places of employment tell us we should love what we do, that we are a family. Why can't we just be happy with what we've been given? Why does work often feel so empty or draining, even if we actually enjoy what we do? We give our employers everything, and at the end of the day, we have nothing left to give ourselves, we have nothing left to give our loved ones.

If our work is meant to be our greatest purpose in life, and we are meant to love our bosses and coworkers like family, then we will devote more of our Self-energy to the work. Self-energy isn't a finite resource, but physical and emotional energy truly is. When we give our work everything, we still only get back our wage in return. Often that wage isn't even enough to live on, while the CEO of the company we work for gets million-dollar bonuses. But capitalism doesn't care about inequity. It tells us that we should care for ourselves through "self-care," which is our sole responsibility, and if we aren't doing it, well, then it's our fault we are broken, tired, burnt-out. Self-care in capitalism often means buying shit we don't need that's probably made overseas in a factory where labor practices are not far off from indentured servitude. Or we "do self-care" by subjecting other people to poor working conditions and exploitation so we can get a cheap massage or manicure. This is capitalism.

My client Aditi grew up in a small, conservative, mostly white Southern town. They had always felt different and like they never belonged. Aditi, like many of my clients, found their belonging only in the woods behind their family's home. They would climb trees for hours, pretending to be a fairy princess or a wizard. They longed for real adventures and, more than anything, wanted to be somewhere they didn't feel so other, or where being other wasn't a bad thing. Toward the end of high school they embraced their queer and nonbinary femme identity. For college they wanted to go where they could be free, where they could be around not just other South Asian folks but other South Asian queers! Aditi found all of that and more in New York City. They found community, identity, culture, and total liberation from the small Southern town mentality they grew up in.

But the pressures from their family to be hypersuccessful as a response to oppression followed them to NYC. This expectation from their parents, aunts and uncles, and cousins wasn't without reason. Aditi had watched everyone in their family work twice as hard for half the amount of money and recognition of their white coworkers. They watched their parents get passed over for promotion after promotion, while younger white cisgender men with half the experience landed the job. While Aditi found the freedom to celebrate their identity in NYC, they couldn't shake the overworking and overachieving that were expected by both their family and the hustle culture of the big city. Aditi told me one day during our session, "Living in New York, I did it all. I got A's in all my classes at NYU, worked a full-time job at a restaurant to pay for rent and food. I would stay up all night dancing with friends at dyke bars and queer dance parties. Then, I would sleep for two or three hours and do it all over again." After college, Aditi went straight into grad school, then straight into their first professional job. They never took time off to "explore" or "adventure" like their white friends did. All of their BIPOC and South Asian friends were just like them, working hard because they had to, partying hard because they were making up for lost time. But there was no time for rest, time off, or slowness. It wasn't an option.

Not long after Aditi landed their first high-paying position that required sixty-to-eighty-hour workweeks, they went on a weekend trip to a gay lodge in the woods with a group of friends. Aditi had never done psychedelics of any kind and was excited to do MDMA together as a group.

For the previous decade, they had been working six days a week.

They had done everything they were "supposed to" do to be successful. Landing that prestigious job was a huge milestone, marking the end of years of barely making rent, juggling working at a restaurant by night with being a student by day to pay bills. They hadn't slowed down to process all that had happened to them since leaving that small Southern town. They had put their nose to the grindstone and done what they needed to do, no matter the cost. That weekend trip with their friends opened their eyes. It took powerful psychedelic drugs for them to wake up and see their life for what it was—missing something very important. They looked out at the forest, its leaves changing with the emergence of fall, rain making the night sky hazy. They realized that while they had, in theory, achieved their dream, they had never felt more disconnected from their core Self. It was as if their Self finally came through the clouds, like the sun breaking through after a thunderstorm. They had been so focused on work, on surviving under capitalism, on trying to prove themselves, that they had lost sight of what they truly wanted. They had to get out of New York City. They had to work less. They had to be closer to nature. They had grown up in the outdoors, and yet they had created a life trapped in the city. How had this happened?

Later, while Aditi was cuddled in bed with friends, a vision came to them. They were standing in their parents' town in India on the bank of the river. They had a heavy pack on their back and were wearing threadbare clothes but they felt happy. The sun shone on their face. They felt connected to Earth and to themselves. They felt free, wild, and totally without destination or purpose, in the best way possible.

One month later, Aditi quit their job. They filled a hiking backpack with clothes, their laptop, and their passport. Aditi was going to see the world. For the literal first time in their adult life, they weren't in school, they didn't have a job. They had enough money to travel on a budget, and knew they could always get another job when they needed to. They told me, "For the first time, my happiness came first. As a kid, all I wanted was to feel free, to feel like I could be myself. I was trying to fit my freedom and my authenticity into the late hours of the night, only to wake up and wear a button-down and a business skirt to work the next day. I knew I had to leave it all behind to really get free." Aditi shares their journey online about how to travel as a queer, brown person. They happily make just enough money off that content creation to keep traveling after their initial savings had run out. They are wild and free.

Capitalism, like trauma, breaks the connection we have with our core Self. Having to work this much and this hard to meet our basic needs leaves no space or time for all those eight C's of Self that we discussed in chapter 4: compassion, curiosity, clarity, creativity, calm, confidence, courage, and connectedness. For Aditi, they experienced a calm and connectedness during their vision about travel that led them, with curiosity, to explore a nonnormative way of living, one that allowed them to feel more aligned with their core Self. Upon awakening, they felt a clarity that the life of hustle and grind was not what they wanted. This required a deep level of self-compassion. Self-compassion to give themselves permission for another life. One where they spent time *not* working, time resting, which Aditi now prioritizes in their travels. Self-compassion for Aditi means telling themselves, "It doesn't have to be so hard," which extends back into their lineage, healing the trauma of generations of ancestors for whom it did have to be that hard, for whom there was no other option.

SELF-COMPASSION

We can't meet capitalism's demands, nor do we want to. We live in a world that consistently tells us that if we aren't producing at a high level, we are not valuable. Therefore, slowing down, resting, and listening to ourselves is powerful resistance. It takes courage to slow down, and confidence and curiosity to listen to your body's needs. The 2020 lockdown created a new phase in our work culture. Younger folks just aren't willing to trade their precious time and bodies for work that they don't enjoy. This is an enormous paradigm shift. But just because things are changing doesn't mean that our inner capitalist can't still get loud, especially when we experience threats to our access to resources. We may feel ready for more rest, slowness, and self-compassion, but the demands of our material reality may say otherwise. Whatever your reality is, whether you want to learn how to slow down and do less and actually can, or your life requires constant work and you want to find more space for rest within it, it is possible to unlearn harmful beliefs and bodily responses and create mismatches to capitalism.

In the chapters on the brain and nervous system, you learned how our body is designed to keep us safe. In a world where our access to life-sustaining resources for physical safety (housing, food, health care, clothing, childcare, medication, and so on) is directly dependent on our ability to make money in the workforce—and where we sometimes spend most of our waking hours working—our bodies are going to have some strong responses to this type of burden. Losing a job, pushing past our body's physical or mental capacities at work, trying to come down from a stressful day—all of these experiences are going to set off internal survival responses. For some of us, working does mean life or death. For others, it doesn't, but our bodies are still telling us it does.

The attention economy[7] functions by turning our leisure time into more production for capitalism. The more we use our devices, the better the algorithms know us, and we can be directed to more marketing through ads and influencers. This makes capitalism inescapable. I show myself self-compassion by unplugging from my devices as often as possible. I am not as aware of world events, and that's okay. I'm not instantly reachable for friends and family, but my loved ones know I love them and that we will connect in more authentic ways than replying to each other on Instagram.

SELF-LIBERATION

Capitalism keeps us oppressed. Every day it seems we are less free to be ourselves. Every day we must work harder to afford to cover our basic needs. We don't experience freedom of our bodies or freedom of our minds when we are so focused on a digital reality that feeds us not what we need to survive but what the system needs to survive.

Healing from our modern world means liberating ourselves. But how can we escape and find ways to experience freedom despite the world we live in? Like Dorothy, who always had the ability to leave Oz and go home, freedom is also within our reach.

The Value of Rest

One of the ways to resist capitalism is rest. In a capitalist society, rest is usually only possible if someone else, someone more marginalized than we are, is completing life tasks for us. Rest is framed as "recharging" so we can go out there and be more productive afterward, a better worker under capitalism.[8]

But what if rest was a time when we could dream of another way of being? Tricia Hersey, founder of the Nap Ministry and author of *Rest Is Resistance*, asks us, What if we rested not to make ourselves better workers, but what if we rested and dreamed just for the sake of rest and dreaming itself? What if dreaming of new worlds during that rest was where the revolution started? Hersey teaches, "Rest is a healing portal to our deepest selves. Rest is care. Rest is radical."[9]

There is such an emphasis on healing as being a verb, something you do actively, that healing work is hard work, just like our jobs. Some of this is true. Therapy, twelve-step programs, educating yourself on trauma—all of these take effort. But what if healing was not work? What if our healing involved doing *less*? What if it is just as radical to stay home and care for our bodies as it is to march in the streets for justice? What if the portal to connecting with our Self again is opened by making space to fully disengage with capitalism and do nothing at all?

After a long day or week of travel, Aditi always makes sure to factor in days to recover, whether it be at a friend's or family member's home or somewhere deep in nature. They can still feel the old call to produce more, to make more content about their travels for more money, or just to "stay busy." Then, they will remind themselves they have what they need, and that rest is how they reconnect with their body and Self.

Connecting with Nature

Another portal to liberation is Earth herself. Some of the most powerful medicine for living in an overdeveloped world and the many traumas related to "modern living" is to spend time with nature, plants, animals, and other humans who deeply love this planet. Nature offers us the healing components of both community and freedom.

We are in community with Earth every day, all day, whether we recognize it or not. Our bodies are nourished by Earth through food, oxygen, and water. We have opportunities throughout our day to feel connected to Earth instead of experiencing the disconnection capitalism breeds. We build community with nature when we acknowledge, witness, and spend time with her, when we notice the birds, the plants, the seasons changing.

For some, connection to nature means practicing close attention,[10] learning the names of the plants and animals in your area and paying attention to them instead of the attention economy of our devices. For others, it's time outdoors, walking, sitting, swimming. I know many people who have felt healed and nourished by helping to build and maintain a community garden. For me, it is simply lying in my backyard, my bare feet in the grass. I feel a deep relationship with the lilac bushes and pine trees in my little urban green space and can feel my body regulating when I am in their presence and even when I view them from a window.

Research shows that time spent in forests or with trees significantly lowers our adrenaline[11] and cortisol levels, reduces our blood pressure, and helps regulate the sympathetic and the parasympathetic nervous system.[12] We quite literally liberate our oppressed bodies when we spend time with nature. It really is that simple.

Co-regulation is the process of regulating our nervous systems with the presence of a calm nervous system of another. Ideally, we experienced this with our caregivers. That being said, many people, like my client Jo, find deep grounding when they are away from other humans and can co-regulate with animals and nature. We all have the ability to co-regulate with nature. Nature can heal our attachment wounds from childhood and create mismatches for our stress-riddled workdays. It is exactly the medicine we need for this "modern world."

Nature doesn't have to mean isolation or spending time in the wilderness. When living in a city, we can still enjoy the earth. Getting outdoors in cities is possible through stoops, parks, rooftops, walks, and opening the windows to hear the birds. Even looking at photos of nature has measurable calming powers for our nervous systems. All of this regulates our nervous system and slows us down from the grind culture that keeps us disconnected from ourselves and from the earth around us.

It's a sad irony that the people who most need the healing experiences of nature may be the ones who have the hardest time reaching her. The lack of green spaces in the most resource-deprived urban areas means that folks who live there must work that much harder to find the respite of nature in their lives. And because they may not have enough time off work and have to travel farther to get access to nature, they have less time to enjoy it. But positive changes are becoming more common in the form of community gardens in neighborhoods that need connection with Earth most.

There was a time in my life when I would not let myself feel the grief of climate change. I had given up on Earth and even said to a friend, "What's the point? Earth is fucked. I'm going to do what I can for people, because that's all we have control over." I had fallen into the colonial bind of believing Earth was separate from myself, from all humans. Instead of sitting with my grief for the planet, I disconnected myself from her as a way to protect myself from pain. I didn't want to recognize how deeply intertwined we all are with this planet, whether we feel it or not.

In the seventeenth century, French philosopher René Descartes put forth the idea of mind-body dualism: that the mind and body are separate—one (the body) is of this world and the other (the mind) is not a physical entity—has fueled our disconnection from our bodies and emotions. The Cartesian Mind-Body dualism is deeply rooted in white, Western, and colonial thinking. We know our minds and bodies are all part of the same being—just think of how our emotional experiences shape our neural pathways, forming beliefs about the world, and how we can physically alter those pathways to create mismatches with previous beliefs. Or how trauma and emotional distress can turn on certain genes, leading to physical pain and illness. Stress itself creates inflammation in the body. Body and mind are certainly one.

Just as our brains and bodies are connected, so are our bodies and Earth. Writer and naturalist Pam Houston says, "The language of the wilderness is the most beautiful language we have and it is our job to sing it, until and even after it is gone, no matter how much it hurts. . . . Yes, the destruction, yes, the inevitability, but honestly, Doctor Distant Reader, when was the last time you slept on the ground?" When we trap ourselves inside, when we avoid feeling grief for Earth or just focus on her destruction, we miss out on the vital medicine of co-regulation she is always offering. But through an honest, deep, raw, and reconnective relationship with Earth, our bodies will experience regulation and our core Self will find the oneness we are meant to have with this planet.

FINDING BALANCE WITHIN COMMUNITY

Community occurs when we care for ourselves and others. The trauma of the "modern world" is not just about surviving capitalism. It is about colonization, climate collapse, genocide, global pandemics, and more. But the sentiment stays the same. As Johanna Hedva writes in their essay "Sick Woman Theory,"[13] "the most anti-capitalist protest is to care for another and to care for yourself." In other words, caring for ourselves and others is a radical act, and community is how we survive our "modern" times. But what does that actually mean? What is the material reality of community care? Of caring for ourselves?

Capitalism and the legacy of colonialism keep us disconnected from one another through an overemphasis on the individual. Capitalism's promise of prosperity for the individual is the opposite of liberation. Individualism keeps our worlds of care small. If we are good, or if we and our immediate partner/family are good, that's all that matters. This is a direct contrast to the notion of collective care. While we are responsible for ourselves to a degree, people need other people. Anyone who has been sick, broke, pregnant, struggling with addiction or mental illness, or in crisis knows this. It is a lot easier to come out on the other side of something with support. Think about the radical act of mutual aid we discussed in chapter 5, where the community steps in to provide for the needs of the individual. Every time we think of others' needs (not instead of our own needs, but in addition to) we lessen the collective load of the traumas of the "modern world." We fight against individualist thinking that keeps us isolated from one another. Considering other people's needs, what would make their bodies and minds feel more comfortable or quite literally able to exist in a space, helps us all feel more cared for and connected to others. (To be clear, caring for others doesn't mean abandoning your self-care in the process. That's codependency—the act of caring for others *instead* of ourselves, which leads to resentment, martyrdom, and a need for control.)[14]

In a world that asks us to constantly abandon ourselves—whether for the sake of our jobs or to people please—it becomes a radical act to listen to our gut, our Self. It is an act of resistance to know our own needs and understand our actual physical, emotional, and psychological capacity. We care for ourselves by saying no, by practicing radical rest, by asking for support when we need it. We care for ourselves by having healthy boundaries with work, and healthy boundaries when caring for others. In this disconnected world, we heal through being in community and doing so in ways that acknowledge our own limits, not override them.

We also care for ourselves by making space for our feelings. We are constantly sitting with the knowledge or violent images of genocide and climate collapse. Instead of holding all of that vicarious trauma inside of us, pretending we are okay, we care for ourselves by stopping what we are doing to scream, cry, grieve. We care for ourselves by working on building self-compassion for the fact that we are living in impossible times, and we are doing our best. This is unlearning hustle culture and decolonizing our minds around what makes us worthy of love and care.

We care by showing up for our bodies when they have needs instead of overriding those needs and continuing to work beyond our capacities. If it feels like we don't have a choice, and many of us don't, then where *do* we have agency? What can we say no to? Where can we ask for support? Where can we slow down and care for ourselves?

Laura van Dernoot Lipsky, founder and director of the Trauma Stewardship Institute and author of *Trauma Stewardship* and *The Age of Overwhelm*, defines those of us impacted by vicarious trauma as "anyone who interacts with the suffering, pain, and crisis of others or our planet." Is this not all of us? Every human on this planet is exposed to the reality of suffering and the climate crisis, whether they look directly at these or not.

The term Lipsky coined, trauma stewardship, describes the process in which those exposed to secondary trauma guide themselves and others gently through the pain and pleasure of existence, staying connected with joy while bearing witness to pain. While this term was created for first responders, therapists, and ecologists witnessing climate change, I want to argue here that we all need to incorporate a process of trauma stewardship into our lives as personal and community care.

Trauma stewardship emphasizes care for others and holding space for their pain and trauma as being a sustainable practice, only made so by slowing down and caring for ourselves versus steamrolling past our bodily and emotional needs. Overriding our warning signals is something capitalism has taught us to do: just keep going, no matter the impact on us. It has no place in community and self-care.

For Aditi, trauma stewardship meant first slowing down and getting out of the rat race of overachieving, overworking, overproducing. Aditi had witnessed immense trauma in their life, watched their parents and small community of other South Asian folks experience violent racism (especially after 9/11), daily microaggressions, and grief at being away from their home country. Aditi had experienced firsthand the macro- and microaggressions of being one of the only not-white students at their grade, middle, and high school. Now, Aditi, in their travels, is able to balance the pain and grief of this world with joy and beauty. When I read their updates, I can feel their happiness radiating from the computer screen. But Aditi shares not just the beautiful, magical moments. They share the challenges and struggles of women and queer and trans folks all over the world. They've organized community-based donations of funds to support people in the Global South who have been the most impacted by colonization. While Aditi has been through a lot and still witnesses so much of the world's pain, they take time to care for themselves and their community. They have found balance, joy, freedom. For me, the concept of trauma stewardship—bearing witness and sharing pain while balancing self-care and rest—best sums up how we survive the trauma of the "modern world."

YOUR TURN

Liberating Yourself from the "Modern World"

In earlier chapters, you learned tools and ideas that can free you from the way the "modern world" endlessly activates your survival responses. Let's explore how to use these tools for healing and liberation.

- Slowing down and noticing that you are in fight or flight is the first step. Notice your nervous system. Think about your window of tolerance and notice if you are outside or inside it. Are you in hypo- or hyperarousal? What tells you that? When your body is telling you it's not safe, remember your Safe Place. Can you show your body it is safe enough?
- The next step is to validate to yourself and your parts that this is how capitalism functions: It keeps us in survival mode so we work like our life depends on it, because for many of us, it does. No, we can't all quit our jobs and focus only on the aspects of life that make us truly happy. We can, however, validate that this isn't okay and society shouldn't be like this instead of dissociating to get through or feeling gaslit by the world all of the time. What parts that you learned about in chapter 4 need love and attention? Is it your inner child or inner teen? Maybe your perfectionist manager part or inner critic are tired and they might like another job. How can you show these parts you've got their backs and you will keep them "safe enough" in these uncertain times? You will always hear them out, not tell them "It's

fine" when it's not, or "Get over it" when they are having a big feeling. You can always meet these parts in your Safe Place for a nurturing space to regulate together and connect.

- And finally: Go outside! Let yourself cry! Allow yourself to feel in whatever way is possible and not overwhelming for you. Capitalism wants us to ignore our bodies and feelings, and every time you check in with yours you are liberating yourself from it, even if just for the moment.

BRINGING IT ALL TOGETHER

How do we heal from the everyday trauma of today's confusing, frightening world? We first need to name that what we are all experiencing is just that, trauma, whether we are directly impacted by it at the moment or witnessing it. We need time in nature, away from our devices and information overload, to let our nervous system settle and recharge. In nature, we experience freedom in our bodies. We need compassion for ourselves, that the demands of capitalism are impossible to meet. We need to stop focusing so hard on making other people happy, to reconnect with our gut, our core Self, and discover our own deep desires for our lives.

We then need to show up for each other and for ourselves. We can do this through mutual aid and time spent regulating with nature. Giving care and accepting care are equally important here. If we heal through mismatches to trauma, then the biggest mismatch we can experience in our isolating and violent world is time feeling peace in our bodies and connection with others.

PART 4

NOW WHAT?

CHAPTER 9

Next Steps on Your Healing Journey

Welcome, friend, to the final chapter of *Healing the Oppressed Body*. In no way is this the end of your journey. While this book has been here for you to help you learn and build tools for self-liberation, it is also a guide to your next steps. Maybe you are ready to find a therapist but want to make sure you are politically aligned. Maybe you love your therapist, but you feel stagnant in your work together. Maybe you need to break up with your therapist but don't know how.

Or perhaps therapy isn't what is accessible or right for you at this time. Then what? What free resources are available to you? What other ways can you heal and reconnect with your core Self? We are going to cover all of this and more in the following pages.

WHAT TYPE OF THERAPY SHOULD I EXPLORE?

In the therapy field, the techniques and methods for treatment that stem from specific theories are called modalities. Some modalities are referred to as evidence-based, which means the results are based on extensive research that can be repeated by other researchers. In therapy, this equates to modalities that have been clinically tested and found to be effective, even for specific mental health issues. Other modalities are referred to as non-evidence-based, meaning they haven't had clinical trials run in a controlled study. Some people feel really strongly about using evidence-based modalities because they are supported by science, and other people see that marker as colonial, as there are many ways of healing that have never been tested in a clinical setting that are very transformative for people.

Below is a list of modalities—some considered evidence-based and some that originate in other ways—that are successful for treating certain mental health issues, and many that can help heal oppression-based trauma.

Talk Therapy

Talk therapy is an umbrella term that includes many different modalities, but at its essence, it is a space for you and a therapist to verbally process and discuss your life, family, feelings, thoughts, and general mental health. In talk therapy, clients are given a space that is just for them to be fully heard. For many people, this process is transformative all on its own. A lot of us don't get the opportunity to have time and space to be listened to and affirmed. And if we didn't get this from our caregivers, then this experience is absolutely going to give us that mismatched experience and rewire our brains and attachment systems. Talk therapy can help us heal from childhood trauma and attachment wounds, and also from any oppression-based traumas. As long as the therapist is aware of oppression and gets it, this is a space in which clients can talk freely and openly about how hard it is to live in a world with severe state repression and violence. Many clients find this type of therapy especially validating when they and the therapist share certain life experiences, like both being trans or

BIPOC. Talk therapy might include psychoanalysis (Freudian analysis, where you lie down on the couch not facing the therapist and free-associate) and relational therapy or relationship-based therapy (where the relationship between the therapist and client becomes a way to process how the client forms and maintains relationships with others). Talk therapy can be done in an office setting, but I have many wonderful colleagues who adapted to COVID by taking these sessions to the park for a "walk and talk session" or just sitting outdoors together. Many therapists meet with clients outside so they can co-regulate with nature. Some talk therapists bring their therapy dogs to sessions for animal co-regulation.

Dialectical Behavior Therapy (DBT)

DBT, created by therapist Marsha Linehan, is a highly structured type of therapy that focuses on building skills of distress tolerance, emotion regulation, mindfulness, and interpersonal effectiveness. DBT includes weekly therapy with a therapist, where the client and therapist focus specifically on the client's life and their application of the skills for their struggles. It also includes group therapy, which is usually the same small group of people who meet each week to work through the modules of DBT skills together with one or two therapists facilitating. DBT may also include a phone coaching session with the therapist during the week for the client, to check in and workshop any issues that have arisen. This modality was designed for people who have borderline personality disorder like Linehan herself but is incredibly effective for anyone who struggles with self-regulation, relationships, and suicidal ideation.

In my opinion, DBT includes some of the best life skills available. Don't we all need more practice tolerating distress, regulating, being mindful, and communicating with others what we need? DBT offers this for those who are really struggling in these areas, as well as anyone who wants to build more self-awareness in these areas of life.

Somatic Therapy

Somatic therapy is the application of the mind-body connection to psychotherapy. Somatic therapy allows us to understand the impact of trauma on our body, assess if we are in our bodies, develop body-based tools for self-regulation, tune in to internal cues and sensations, and, in some cases, safely process trauma verbally and/or through the body. This type of therapy is very experiential, with the therapist and client talking less and instead noticing physical sensations to feel present in their bodies and release tension. Some psychotherapists are trained in types of somatic therapy that involve touch, the use of light touch or physical guidance by the therapist. Other types of somatic therapy do not include touch. This is a very personal choice for both therapist and client. Some types of somatic therapy are offered by licensed practitioners who are not psychotherapists, like massage therapists. Some people prefer not to be touched by a psychotherapist and prefer to do somatic therapy with a bodyworker.

Somatic therapy can be a useful tool if you want to be more in touch with your body, learn to manage dissociation, feel more regulated in your nervous system, and process trauma using your body, so the body can feel safe and like it belongs to you once again.

Somatic modalities include:

1. **Somatic Experiencing (SE)** is a type of somatic therapy that helps clients understand their own body sensations and how their bodies process a specific trauma physically. Practitioners are trained to help the body release physiological stress responses that prevent psychological healing from a traumatic event or a

lifetime of trauma. Many SE practitioners are also trained in touch work—where the therapist touches the client's body to release pent-up energy from the trauma. SE practitioners can be psychotherapists, massage therapists, or somatic coaches. Massage therapists do bodywork in ways therapists can't because they are trained to safely and effectively work with the physical body and touch. That being said, massage therapists don't have the same training in clinical mental health skills.

Either way, I suggest finding someone trained in a somatic modality and licensed as a psychotherapist or a massage therapist, versus someone who is a somatic coach and hasn't received the same amount of training or isn't held to a professional standard, because a lot can come up when we are working with the body, and you want to be in competent hands. If someone advertises that they are a somatic therapist but does not specify what kind, it is reasonable to ask what they are trained in and what you can expect from somatic therapy with them. Anyone can say they are a somatic coach without necessarily having the training to back it up!

2. **Eye Movement Desensitization and Reprocessing (EMDR):** We delved into EMDR in chapter 2. This modality may be for you if you want to reprocess traumatic memories and have struggled with talk therapy in the past. EMDR is also a somatic modality, meaning it incorporates the body into the processing. EMDR therapists must be licensed mental health practitioners who have completed EMDR basic training and the required consultation hours. Many EMDR therapists continue their training onward to become certified in EMDR, which means they have been trained in applying EMDR to a specialized issue like PTSD, dissociation, parts work, and more.

   In the therapeutic setting, clients are invited to notice the thoughts that come up between sets of bilateral stimulation (BLS), which is when the right side then the left side of the body are stimulated in turn, either through movements of the eyes, headphones that beep in the left ear then the right ear, bilateral tapping of the hands on the knees or chest, or tapping the feet on the ground. Simply talking engages the thinking brain, but when we are asked to slow down and experience BLS with our body, we get more mindful. Essentially, BLS allows processing to take place effectively and safely in an embodied way. It allows our brain to make new connections, faster.

Some people believe that EMDR might be too intense and overwhelming, that it's exposure therapy for trauma, or that it means fully reliving a traumatic memory in order to process it. In fact, the opposite is true. EMDR is a gentle and effective method for treating trauma that works with mental snapshots of past traumas, and it should never be overwhelming. If it is overwhelming for the client, the therapist needs to slow down the work, or maybe the client needs to find a therapist who goes slower.

3. **EMDR Reverse Protocol:** There are some people who have tried processing childhood trauma in talk therapy, and maybe even somatic therapy like EMDR or SE, but found it overwhelming and triggering. Some people might also be terrified to begin to process trauma because it feels like it would uproot their entire lives. My response: Try an EMDR technique called reverse protocol.

   With EMDR reverse protocol, we can still get at the hub of the impact of the trauma without going into it directly with memories. The EMDR reverse protocol asks us to look at fears for the future related to the trauma instead of the actual trauma memory itself. Typically, fears people have for the future include "I'll be alone," or "I'll be broken and never heal." Sometimes these fears are just as upsetting as the memories from childhood, but the content of the fear isn't as distressing. It can be a more tolerable approach for some. When we process the impact of the abuse and fear (being alone, feeling broken), we address the same feelings we most likely had during the abuse itself. Clients who have done reverse protocol often feel as though they have processed their childhood trauma without getting overwhelmed. Some may end up processing those memories, but by the time they do so, they have processed the fears and present-day triggers so the childhood memories don't feel as intense.

This technique is also useful for people who have no emotions associated with their trauma memories or no memories of the trauma itself, because of dissociation or because trauma happened so long ago and they have "known" about these memories for so long that there's really no emotional charge there. Clients may still desire to process this trauma even though it is not very distressing, as that lack of emotional charge tends to be due to dissociation. And when that dissociation spills over into the rest of their lives, it keeps them stuck in "not feeling" mode. This can limit their emotions about the rest of their lives, not only their trauma.

There are a number of other EMDR protocols that can be utilized for complex trauma. (Note: If you want to process childhood trauma more deeply but fear that it will be totally dysregulating, make sure you find a therapist with a focus in cPTSD who is trained in these protocols. It will make an enormous difference.)

Internal Family Systems (IFS)

By this point in the book, you are an expert in IFS. If the approach really resonated with you, it might be a modality you want to explore in therapy. IFS is a gentle and expansive way of working with trauma. It does not have to be used just for trauma treatment, though. IFS is a beautiful way of going deeper into therapy and getting to know yourself on a new level. It can be flexible and isn't highly structured. In IFS therapy, you get to know your parts, working with protectors to help them step back and take on a new role in your system so that you can unburden exiles from their pain and trauma. I find IFS to be most useful for clients who want to change how they see themselves or speak to themselves. IFS encourages love and acceptance of all parts, and I watch with my clients how they immediately start viewing their actions, thoughts, and feelings with more kindness as soon as I introduce the concept. That being said, IFS is not the only modality that looks at parts of self. General parts work, reparenting yourself, ego-state therapy, and Jungian analysis all do so as well. Parts theory has been used in psychotherapy since its conception.

I've witnessed IFS and other parts-work modalities as being really healing for the following: addiction (in combination with a twelve-step program), cPTSD, attachment wounding, eating disorders, self-harm, and suicidal ideation. IFS can be used in conjunction with talk therapy or somatic therapy—honestly any type of therapeutic modality. It is incredibly applicable across the board. I personally use IFS along with EMDR using an EMDR and IFS protocol and have found that this approach deepens the EMDR therapy I do with clients tremendously.

Today, only licensed therapists can get trained in IFS. But until recently, IFS training was open to life coaches and other practitioners, so make sure the person you're working with is a licensed mental health practitioner if that is important to you. Licensed therapists have more training than life coaches and have a code of ethics they have to abide by, unlike coaches. Coaching can be really helpful for other life issues, but when it comes to deep trauma work, I again suggest seeing a licensed therapist.

Cognitive Behavioral Therapy (CBT)

CBT gets a bad rap these days, and sometimes for a good reason. CBT posits that if you change the way you think, it will change the way you feel, and in turn, change the way you behave in life. It helps shift your brain's perceptions, which can be extremely helpful for those of us whose brains get stuck in certain ways of thinking, ruminating, and worrying. CBT is effective for certain kinds of mental health issues, including depression, insomnia, hairpulling, skin picking, phobias, personality disorders, eating disorders, body dysmorphic disorder, OCD, and some presentations of anxiety. The reason CBT is helpful is that these issues can be powerfully resolved or lessened by cognitive thought work, and in fact, doing only body-based therapy can make some of these issues *worse*. I know clients who have spent years in therapy doing somatic work or parts work, when all along what they really needed to resolve their anxiety or OCD was some good old-fashioned CBT! Other types of therapy can exacerbate symptoms or keep someone stuck, as sessions are used for reassurance, not for rewiring a person's brain, which people with generalized anxiety disorder (GAD), phobias, social anxiety disorder, and OCD really need. CBT includes many different types of evidence-based practices, and each one tends to be extensively tested as treatment for its specific mental health issue. CBT is also highly effective right away; I have seen clients get relief from just a few sessions.

However, CBT can be invalidating for PTSD, cPTSD, grief, stress, the trauma of systemic oppression, and *some* types of neurodivergence like autism. The reason it doesn't work for these experiences is that they each have a lived reality. To imply that these psychological conditions are due to just your beliefs about the world and that your thinking is the problem invalidates the pain and stress that is real in your life and body and belittles your life experience. Trying to change our thinking to heal trauma, grief, stress, and experiences of oppression can lead to feeling that we shouldn't be feeling our feelings, which can make us feel worse. It's kind of like when people say, "You're safe now! Move on!" or "Well, that was in the past, why are you still upset?" If it were that simple, we would have moved on. But these experiences impact our bodies on the nervous-system level, as well as our internal relationship to our core Self and our parts.

Exposure and Response Prevention (ERP)

ERP is the go-to treatment for OCD, phobias, avoidant/restrictive food intake disorder (ARFID), social anxiety, and eating disorders. ERP is a type of CBT therapy. When it is done correctly, the therapist and client work together to build a fear hierarchy. At the bottom, where you would begin with your therapist, is the least distressing exposure to your fear or least distressing experiment with *not* doing a safety behavior—a compulsion like checking, asking for reassurance, or even ruminating about something. You and the therapist slowly work your way up the hierarchy until you face the hardest experience, gradually teaching your brain and nervous system that it is actually okay or safe, and you can handle it. Clients practice with exposure both inside and outside of therapy sessions.

An example of this would be a fear of flying. For people with this type of phobia the brain has fused the idea of flying in a plane with crashing. At the bottom of the pyramid could be talking about flying, thinking about booking a trip, or looking at photos of planes. The middle of the pyramid might be going to the airport to watch the planes, or even discussing or imagining plane crashes. At the top of the fear hierarchy could be looking at photos or even videos of plane crashes, imagining being in a plane crash, or taking a flight somewhere. This approach sounds really intense, and like it could be traumatizing or upsetting for someone. But when done correctly, the fear hierarchy is advanced at a steady and slow pace so it isn't overwhelming for the client. This approach helps the brain defuse the connection between flying and dying. For any other kind of fear or OCD obsession, exposing the brain to gradually increased perceived threat helps the person face the imagined outcome straight on, and the body has less of a fight-or-flight response to the fear each time, habituating to the thing they are most scared of until it becomes mostly benign.

Inference-Based Cognitive Behavioral Therapy (I-CBT)

I-CBT is an emerging treatment modality for OCD, body dysmorphic disorder (BDD), and social anxiety. It is a nonexposure-based treatment that looks at the dysfunctional reasoning behind obsessive thinking and how OCD hijacks our brain and nervous system. I-CBT offers concrete tools to learn to come back to reality and away from the imaginative pull of OCD. This is the modality I use in my practice for OCD, and you can learn more about this modality at icbt.online.

Psychedelic-Assisted Therapy

As I write this, I feel hopeful that we sit on the precipice of a new age in treatment for trauma. Here's why: This book has been devoted to learning about how corrective emotional experiences can rewire the brain, and how the repetition of those experiences is what changes and creates new neural networks. Psychedelic-assisted therapy may work by opening neural pathways more easily and solidify them more rapidly.[1] Similar to the research findings on EMDR, psychedelic-assisted therapy may help maladaptive networks die off or be rerouted (think of those hiking paths!) so new connections can be made. However, psychedelics appear to stimulate these changes at a much faster rate.

Take Aditi, for example. While they did MDMA with friends (not in a controlled therapeutic environment), they had realizations and revelations that may have taken much longer without the assistance of the drugs. Their new understanding allowed them to make changes in their life.

With psychedelics, people may experience neural changes that would take years to reach in traditional therapy—if at all. I suggest the podcast *Inside Eyes* with host Laura Mae Northrup to learn more. In some states, ketamine-assisted therapy is available now. There are many survivors of trauma, as well as doctors, scientists, and therapists, who are working hard to get MDMA and psilocybin legalized for therapeutic use as well.

FINDING A THERAPIST WHO GETS YOU

While the type of therapy you decide to do is important, finding the right therapist to work with is just as vital for healing.

One of the most common issues I hear from clients is that their previous therapists didn't understand them. This can happen when a therapist and client don't share any of the same identities and the client feels like they have to educate the therapist. So many queer, trans, and BIPOC clinicians are now entering the field, so you have more options to work with someone who shares identities that are important to you.

When you are searching for a therapist on a platform like Psychology Today, you can select areas the person specializes in and even some identities they hold. Most therapists offer a free consultation to meet them, which is not just for them to ask you questions but also for you to interview them. It is reasonable to ask about their experience with certain groups of people, and whether they belong to those groups. As a potential client, you have the right to know if a therapist is able to hold the complexities of your life from firsthand experience, so you can feel held and understood by someone who has been there too. And if the therapist hasn't been in your shoes, you can ask what work they've done to understand someone like you. As our culture has shifted, it has become more clinically acceptable and even necessary for therapists to disclose an appropriate amount of personal information so clients can make the best choice about working with us. As more therapists who hold complex identities have begun working in the field, there is a recognition that being forthcoming about our identities can influence the therapeutic relationship. I know many friends and also clients who have strict qualifications for their therapist: They must share an identity or life experience, like "must be a person of color" or "must be trans." When you are reading a therapist's website or profile, you can often glean some of their political beliefs and values. Feel empowered to ask more direct questions in the short call before scheduling. It may be really important to you that your therapist has an understanding of your belief system, and that is valid and okay. If they don't, or if they don't share all or some of your identities, sit with what they are offering and what their experience is.

In my twenties it was vital for me to have a fellow dyke therapist, and my relationship with them really did change my life *because* they were queer. But I have not had a queer therapist since then. The therapists I have worked with I picked more for their therapeutic modalities and the fact that they took my health insurance. The issues we are working on together don't have to do with my queerness, and they are good queer allies. It's no longer the most important qualifier for me.

If you begin meeting with someone and it doesn't feel like the right fit, don't let the sunk-cost fallacy fool you! Staying isn't always the thing that is best just because you already got started. You don't have to stay with someone just because you did their intake and initial few sessions. You don't owe that person anything other than a courteous email. But before you leave the therapist, see if it feels possible to discuss why you think it's not working for you. This is a great opportunity to safely practice unlearning people pleasing! If it doesn't feel safe to do so, just move on. I'll give you some help on how to know when it's time to leave in a moment. But first, let's address the elephant in the room: the cost of therapy.

AFFORDABILITY

Therapy can be costly, largely due to all the overhead costs that therapists have to cover: trainings, malpractice insurance, supervision, license fees, and office rent and overhead if they see clients in person. And many group practices don't offer health insurance or benefits like paid time off, sick pay, and parental leave. So we tend to charge the amount we need to sustain all of that.

If the therapist you like doesn't take your insurance, make sure you are receiving superbills (receipts with your diagnosis code and the type of service you received), which you can submit for out-of-network benefits. Some insurance plans will start to cover sessions after you hit a deductible or will cover a percentage of them. You can also use money in a health savings account (HSA) to pay for sessions. If sessions with the person you want to work with aren't affordable, ask if they offer sliding-scale fees or have a waitlist for sliding scale.

Check out Open Path Collective for therapists who charge between thirty and seventy dollars per session.

If you are using your insurance plan for therapy, you can plug your insurance network right into the filters on your search. This will populate therapists who take your insurance. You can also search for therapy clinics that take your insurance and offer the type of modality that you are looking for. There also might be nonprofits in your area that offer free, low-cost, or in-network therapy. If your search turns up a group practice, you may not get to pick the specific therapist you work with, but it could still be a good fit. If it isn't, ask to be transferred to a different therapist who might better fit what you are looking for. Clinics tend to have high turnover because they don't pay therapists very much, and they staff interns who are still in counseling school doing their practicum at the site, but these therapists are typically younger, getting trained, and really excited about the work. You might even follow them to their own practices someday.

Here are some good places to search for a therapist:

- Psychology Today
- Alma (most therapists on this platform take insurance)
- Open Path Collective (sliding scale)
- Manhattan Alternative (directory of affirming therapists for queer, trans, poly, and kink identities)
- EMDR International Association (directory of fully trained EMDR therapists)
- International OCD Foundation

DECIDING TO STAY OR GO

If your current therapist isn't meeting your needs, it can be hard to leave. Or, if you stay, it can be hard to advocate for your needs to be better met. Here are some reasons you might feel things need to change:

- You don't feel like your therapist understands you, that you have to explain your life and educate them on basic identity information
- You feel that you aren't focusing on your goals for therapy
- There isn't enough structure to sessions
- Your therapist isn't trained in a modality you want to try and feel would better serve your goals for therapy
- Your therapist only offers remote therapy, and you do better with an in-person connection
- Your therapist only does in-person, but you prefer to do therapy from home and/or where it's more accessible for you
- Your therapist shares too much about their personal life
- Your therapist seems influenced by a religion, spirituality, or belief system you don't subscribe to
- You and your therapist don't have a good connection or good rapport
- You feel stuck without change or improvement for a long period of time, despite implementing tools from therapy and attending regularly

Even if you feel any of the above, there are some reasons you might decide to stay and work on it:

- **Your therapist is open to feedback and asks you frequently how sessions are feeling or checks in with your goals.** In this scenario, I suggest using that time to voice how you feel and see if it's something that could be worked out within the relationship.
- **Your therapist is trained in the modality you are interested in; they just aren't using it.** I hear about this issue often. Sometimes therapists struggle to implement modalities they are trained in. Shar-

ing that you're interested in EMDR, IFS, or DBT, or that you want more structure in sessions could help the two of you come up with a therapy plan that better meets your needs.

- **You have switched between many therapists and modalities, and are seeing no improvement.** Sometimes we feel that the next therapist will be the one to "heal us" or that a new modality is going to be the one to really make change in our life. When we switch between too many providers and modalities, we never get to complete one or create enough of a relationship with one person to go deep. Give a few months to one therapist and modality, as long as there are no major issues with either. It can take time.
- **Your therapist is meeting some of your needs but not all. For example, they are also trans but not trained in the type of therapy you need. Or they are trained in that modality but seem to lack understanding of trans life experiences.** Ask if your therapist is willing to get some training or consultation that would help them better understand you or meet your needs. Therapists have to complete hours and hours of continuing education credits, and many are looking for more ways to better serve their clients. If they are willing, it might just be a daylong training or some time working with a supervisor to become the therapist you need. If they are not willing to get additional training, that is confirmation that they are not the right person for you.

What if it really is time to go? What if you and your therapist have tried to make it work, but they just aren't the right fit, identity- and/or modality-wise? What if you are now realizing that your difference in worldview has limited your ability to be understood or maybe even heal fully? What if you have realized you have a diagnosis that your therapist doesn't know about and can't get training soon enough to provide what you need?

Technically, you don't "owe" your therapist a termination session. Meeting once more to end the relationship should be done if it would be healing, reparative, or offer closure for *you*. Sometimes we might feel avoidant of a final session, especially if we have strong people pleaser parts. It might seem easier to ghost them or end the relationship over email. Check in with your parts about who is showing up around ending the relationship, and what your core Self ultimately needs for this end to be a mismatch to past experiences. Have you typically let relationships go on for longer than they needed to? Have you historically ghosted someone when it might have been a growth moment for you to face them and say what you feel? Either way, it's up to you if you want to share with a therapist why you are ending the relationship.

SUPPORTIVE HEALING OPTIONS OTHER THAN THERAPY

Therapy isn't for everyone. It can be inaccessible. For some it's off the table for reasons of historical trauma. It may be something that you were forced to do as a child or as part of a program and therefore is not something you feel interested in doing right now. The good news is there are other ways of healing that can be as or more effective than therapy or that, combined with therapy, can make any self-work you are doing more impactful and healing. Let's look at some other options besides psychotherapy.

Twelve-Step Recovery Programs

Alcoholics Anonymous (AA) and its sister programs have helped millions of people worldwide. While some folks swear by them, others are wary because of the many misconceptions about the programs, such as their use of a higher power or, for some, God. Let's take a look at some of the myths that may stand in the way of making use of this powerful, effective (and free) path to healing.

- **Myth #1: Twelve-step programs aren't for marginalized groups.** If you are looking for a specific space, one that is queer-only, trans-only, or BIPOC-only, simply apply that filter when searching for a meeting on any of their websites, and you will eventually find a group that is right for you.
- **Myth #2: Twelve-step programs are religious.** In twelve-step programs, people pray. There is work done to cultivate a relationship to a higher power. This myth exists because people associate both of these with God, and therefore, with a religious environment. It doesn't help that many meetings take place in the basement of churches, and in some more religious areas, the meeting is closed out with both the Serenity Prayer *and* the Lord's Prayer. But *higher power* doesn't have to mean God. Higher power literally means a power greater than you. I know someone whose higher power is Britney Spears. My higher power is nature. When I pray to nature, I am not praying to God. Most people, atheist or not, do not believe they are the ultimate most powerful being or energy in the universe. All twelve-step programs ask you to do is acknowledge that. If religious environments are triggering, definitely don't go to a meeting in a church. It's as simple as that. If the meeting has a vibe you don't like, try others until you find one that fits your needs.
- **Myth #3: Twelve-step programs shame people with addiction.** Calling oneself an addict or alcoholic (as in, "Hi, I'm Andrea, and I'm an alcoholic") is a way of destigmatizing, not stigmatizing, addiction. It can actually be very freeing for folks. In twelve-step programs, addiction is seen as a disease, not as something to be ashamed of. At the same time, though, members are held accountable for their actions.

Addiction as a disease doesn't mean you get a free pass to do whatever you want or not make amends. No one is shamed; everyone is accountable.

- **Myth #4: Twelve-step programs are only for people with substance use issues.** Twelve-step programs—each with their own unique meetings, books, and steps—exist not only for most addictions but also for major issues most human beings deal with like codependency (Co-dependents Anonymous, or CoDA), growing up in a dysfunctional home (Adult Children of Alcoholics and Dysfunctional Families, or ACA), and loving someone with an addiction (Al-Anon). Who among us doesn't struggle with codependency? Who among us has not grown up in a home that was dysfunctional in some way? Who among us has not loved someone with an addiction? There are many more twelve-step groups, but I mention these three because they're the ones I suggest the most to clients.

Twelve-step recovery programs are unparalleled in their ability to help people heal from addiction. The programs are free and, in my opinion, when coupled with therapy or even on their own are an incredibly effective treatment for childhood trauma. In these programs you can work the steps just like someone who is recovering from an addiction. The steps are a process of unburdening from childhood, letting go of maladaptive coping learned in dysfunctional childhoods, and building trust and intimacy with your group and sponsor. It is some of the most profound healing work available to us, and now meetings are both in-person and remote.

For a full list of twelve-step programs, check out 12step.com/12stepprograms.

Meetings directories can be found on each program's website (aa.org, coda.org, etc.). Use the filter just like you would while searching for a therapist. You can search for meetings that are in-person near you or online, or specify ones that are queer-only, women-only, POC-only, or all of the above!

Movement

Somatic therapy isn't the only way for us to deepen our relationship with our bodies. Many of my clients find healing and embodiment when they engage in movement like yoga, dance, kickboxing, rock climbing, hiking, pole dancing, and more. Sometimes this practice is done alone at home, and other times in structured classes. Sometimes beautiful communities are built around a movement class or space. A lot of people find these practices to be gender-affirming, body-affirming, and a good way to work stress, trauma, and tension out of their bodies. Movement is healing when it is done as an act of love for one's body, not out of trying to change or conform it.

If you are considering entering a space that offers movement classes, it is common to have some reservations or concerns. Similar to finding the right therapist, finding the right teacher or studio can take a period of trial and error. I suggest shopping around and trying out a few different options before committing. You can often tell by the language on the website and by who works at a studio if you will feel welcome there, but you can always call ahead with questions. I also encourage you to feel empowered to leave a class or space if your body doesn't feel safe or welcomed there or if the language is too body-negative.

Sex

As we discussed in chapter 5, healing can happen in community through sex. Consensual sex can be especially liberating for those who have experienced religious trauma or any oppression-based trauma.

Queer sex can be a mismatch in so many ways. Many of my trans clients and loved ones experience gender euphoria during sex with other trans folks. To freely experience sex is a radical act of self-liberation in a world that deems you wrong, disgusting. Specifically, kink and BDSM, which can be uniquely healing for those suffering from chronic pain or illness as a way to build a new relationship to pain, one that is their choice, one that is pleasure-based and not within a medical system. Kink can offer corrective emotional experiences. Essentially, a mismatch. *I was oppressed, and in kink I am liberated. I was shamed for my sexuality, and now I am celebrated. I had no power, and now I have power. I didn't choose it and now I get to choose it.* So anytime we have the opposite experience, our nervous system experiences healing.

Other Embodiment Techniques

Anything that gets you into your body can be healing. This might be through body modification such as tattoos and piercings or self-expression and affirmation through makeup and clothing (turning a look) or public performances like karaoke, drag, and poetry readings. Many of my clients feel embodied when taking to the streets during a march or protest, even though these political acts can sometimes make people feel activated or expose them to aggression. Being in a crowd of people, feeling your rage, and standing up for what you believe in can be incredibly healing.

Books

Books on healing, recovery, and therapy are fantastic ways to build skills and understanding about our bodies, trauma, and really any emotional issue we are having in our lives. Below are some of my recommended books, organized by subject.

Trauma and Generational Trauma:

- *My Grandmother's Hands: Racialized Trauma and the Pathway to Mending Our Hearts and Bodies* by Resmaa Menakem, MSW, LICSW, SEP
- *Liberation Psychology: Theory, Method, Practice, and Social Justice*, edited by Lillian Comas-Díaz and Edil Torres Rivera
- *Break the Cycle: A Guide to Healing Intergenerational Trauma* by Dr. Mariel Buqué
- *Transforming the Living Legacy of Trauma: A Workbook for Survivors and Therapists* by Janina Fisher, PhD
- *Decolonizing Therapy: Oppression, Historical Trauma, and Politicizing Your Practice* by Jennifer Mullan, PsyD
- *Who is Wellness For? An Examination of Wellness Culture and Who It Leaves Behind* by Fariha Róisín

Traumas of the Modern World and Healing Through Nature:

- *Saving Time: Discovering a Life Beyond Productivity Culture* by Jenny Odell
- *How to Do Nothing: Resisting the Attention Economy* by Jenny Odell
- *Emergent Strategy: Shaping Change, Changing Worlds* by adrienne maree brown
- *Braiding Sweetgrass: Indigenous Wisdom, Scientific Knowledge, and the Teachings of Plants* by Robin Wall Kimmerer

Parts Work and IFS:

- *No Bad Parts: Healing Trauma and Restoring Wholeness with the Internal Family Systems Model* by Richard C. Schwartz, PhD
- *The Loving Parent Guidebook: The Solution Is to Become Your Own*

Loving Parent, from the Adult Children of Alcoholics/Dysfunctional Families World Services Organization
- *Self-Therapy: A Step-By-Step Guide to Creating Inner Wholeness Using IFS, a New, Cutting-Edge Therapy* by Jay Earley, PhD
- *Radical Compassion: Learning to Love Yourself and Your World with the Practice of RAIN* by Tara Brach

cPTSD and Codependency:

- *Homecoming: Reclaiming and Healing Your Inner Child* by John Bradshaw
- *The Complex PTSD Workbook: A Mind-Body Approach to Regaining Emotional Control and Becoming Whole* by Arielle Schwartz, PhD
- *The Drama of the Gifted Child: The Search for the True Self* by Alice Miller
- *Codependent No More: How to Stop Controlling Others and Start Caring for Yourself* by Melody Beattie
- *Are You My Mother? A Comic Drama* by Alison Bechdel
- *Set Boundaries, Find Peace: A Guide to Reclaiming Yourself* by Nedra Glover Tawwab
- *Leaving the Fold: A Guide for Former Fundamentalists and Others Leaving Their Religion* by Marlene Winell, PhD

Burnout:

- *Burnout: The Secret to Solving the Stress Cycle* by Emily and Amelia Nagoski
- *Trauma Stewardship: An Everyday Guide to Caring for Self While Caring for Others* by Laura van Dernoot Lipsky with Connie Burk
- *Rest Is Resistance: A Manifesto* by Tricia Hersey

The Brain, Neuroplasticity, and Neurodiversity:

- *Bouncing Back: Rewiring Your Brain for Maximum Resilience and Well-Being* by Linda Graham, MFT
- *Seven and a Half Lessons About the Brain* by Lisa Feldman Barrett
- *Unmasking Autism: The Power of Embracing Our Hidden Neurodiversity* by Dr. Devon Price

OCD and Anxiety:

- *"Pure O" OCD: Letting Go of Obsessive Thoughts with Acceptance and Commitment Therapy* by Chad Lejeune, PhD
- *Relationship OCD: A CBT-Based Guide to Move Beyond Obsessive Doubt, Anxiety, and Fear of Commitment in Romantic Relationships* by Sheva Rajaee, MFT
- *Overcoming Body-Focused Repetitive Behaviors: A Comprehensive Behavioral Treatment for Hair Pulling and Skin Picking* by Charles S. Mansueto, PhD, Sherrie Mansfield Vavrichek, LCSW-C, and Ruth Goldfinger Golomb, LCPC
- *Resolving OCD: Understanding Your Obsessional Experience* by Frederick Aardema, PhD

This is by no means a comprehensive list of all the books on healing, but it includes some of my personal favorites and ones that have deeply inspired this book.

Epilogue

GOODBYE FOR NOW

What a journey we have been on together. Throughout the book you have been building skills for creating mismatches: giving your brain, body, and parts a new experience through compassion, community, and freedom. You've learned to show compassion for your body, your nervous system, your ancestors, your communities, and all inner parts of yourself. You've learned how to find community with all parts of your inner self, as well as with peer groups, microcommunities, and the natural world around you. You've learned that freedom in your body can be found in sex, movement, creativity, activism, and, again, being with nature. And freedom of your thoughts and actions can be achieved through mindfulness and all the ways we have learned to retrain your brain and soothe your nervous system. It is the repetition of new experiences that rewires your brain and your attachment system. This is no false promise—everything you have learned here really has the potential to help you build new neural connections and pathways in your brain.

Healing from oppression-based trauma really is a radical act of self-liberation. And I want to end this book with a call to action. Our individual healing *is* collective healing, and our collective healing transforms us on a personal level. There is not one without the other. The work you do on yourself, whether inside the therapy room or a twelve-step meeting, or working through a book like this, has a ripple effect throughout your community, family (whoever you consider that to really be!), and the entire world. This isn't hyperbolic; this is how we heal this broken world and its corrupt systems. At the same time, the work you do in your communities, the consciousness you raise, the mutual aid you provide heals you too. Our healing is intricately bound up in one another's, and I believe with my whole self that, as poet and activist Emma Lazarus wrote in 1883, "Until we are all free, we are none of us free."

We have reached the end of *Healing the Oppressed Body*, and from the bottom of my big gay heart, I hope you have found something useful, resonant, or validating here. Take what you need and leave the rest!

Thank you for joining me on this journey!

ACKNOWLEDGMENTS

I never understood what people meant when they would open their acknowledgments with "This book is only possible because of you," but the team of incredible women I have had the honor to work with on this project has shown me what that statement means. I offer my deepest gratitude to the following powerhouse women. First, to Georgia Frances King, for finding my website and believing I could write something like this. This book *literally* only exists because of you. To my agent, Laura Nolan, who saw this project and knew what it needed to be way before I did. Thank you for seeing me, and seeing this book for what it should be. Thank you for your relentless work in getting it published and making sure it was honored for what it's worth. To my editor, Lilly Golden, your kindness, talent, and sharp eye never cease to amaze me. The moment we met, I knew you were the only person who could transform this book into what it needed to be. Thank you for your patience with my run-on sentences, your curiosity, your skills, and your investment in getting this book out to our communities. You are the best of the best. To Meg Leder, my editor at Penguin Life, thank you for taking me and this book seriously. Thank you for your discerning eye and brilliant mind. I still can't believe you picked me.

To my previous supervisor and colleague Malwina Andruczyk, LCSW, your generosity and guidance was the light in the darkness, and it saved me. I am honored to know you and be your friend. To my EMDR consultant, Cristina Smugala, LPC, thank you for your knowledge, your kindness, and your genius. I can't believe I get to work with such a powerhouse, and one as attuned and gentle as you. To my college professors Drs. T. L. Cowan, Jasmine Rault, Kate Eichhorn, and Pooja Rangan. You opened my eyes to the world, radicalized me, and guided me. Thank you for everything, and I hope you can hear all you taught me in these pages. I am forever grateful.

To mi hermana, B. Ruiz, LCSW, thank you for showing me that lesbian motherhood was possible. Thank you for being just as loud and neurotic as me. Thank you for surviving so we could meet each other and be sisters. To Fawzy Qamar, I loved you from the moment I saw you. Thank you for loving *me* through the messy years, and through every new chapter since. You understand me in a way no one else does, or ever will. To Felicia Rosemary, my first project in college was to make you my friend, and it worked. Thank you for showing me the light, for walking into sobriety together. Thank you for believing in me as a writer. To Aubrey Dribben, thank you for two decades of friendship. Here we are, twenty years later, therapists and mothers. Here's to the next twenty. To Alex Hope, Mars Hobrecker, and Glossy Bohemond for your patience and love as we navigated being baby queers together. To Caitlin Rose, for holding me through the same messy years, and for the magic. To the Heels on Wheels femmes, thank you for the adventure and for the world-building. I learned so much from you all. To my wife's best friends: Jo, Andrew, Wren, and Hannah, thank you for loving me and adopting me as a friend—I would choose you on my own.

To my aunt Desiree for wanting to have the deep relationship that we have built, and for helping birth my child. I know in my heart

I had the positive experience that I did because of you. I will never stop thanking you for that. To mi prima, Eva Sanchez, I love all that we share and how we have both dedicated our lives to radical liberation. You are my rock in our extended family. To both of my sisters-in-law, Sara and Carly, for your unwavering support. To my in-laws for every single thing you did to bring and keep my beloved in this world, I will never take for granted how you fought for her. Susan, thank you for your frequency and depth of care and support. I am so grateful for every single thing you do.

To my brother, Jeremy, my life would be incomplete without you. Our parents wanted you to be, but I think I wanted you even more. I love how tender, how passionate, and how grounded of a person you are. To my father, Jeffrey, thank you for growing into the father I needed you to be. Thank you for pushing me to become independent, and for your endless support through my entire life. To my mother, Dr. Rachel Glik, where do I begin? I have everything I have because of you, starting with my brain, my nervous system, and my sense of self. You loved me into existence. Thank you for pushing me (gently) into this field. I love my job every single day because of you. I will only say this once, but you were right! Thank you and Dad for delighting and caring for my child with the same delight and care I take. I *never* take that or you two for granted. To my grandmother Eileen Tamsky, LCSW, who worked at Planned Parenthood for over forty years, you *literally* paved the way. You are an icon and a legend, and everyone should know your name. Thank you for all you have given our family, and this world.

To those who are no longer here: my grandfathers Joseph Glik and Morris Tamsky. How did I get the two most gentle, kind, and smart grandfathers? Your sacrifices gave me the beautiful life I have, and I will tell your stories to my children and my children's children, para siempre. To my grandmother Gussie Glik, I never got to meet you, but I know we are the same. Thank you for my hips and for my brazen, stubborn personality. To my cousin Charlie Glik, you are not forgotten. To my dear friend Thomas Baggett, not a day goes by that I don't want to pick up the phone and tell you about my life.

To my ancestors who came before me, who literally scratched and clawed to survive in hopes that I might, and my children might, have a different life. I will never know how much you gave and all you went through, but I think of it constantly. I feel you beside me, inside me, and with me. Thank you for your insistence on living, your devotion to radical politics (Socialismo o muerte!), and your love of all things beautiful, even as your lives were uncertain and unsafe. I still have so much to learn from you all.

To my wife, Dr. Katherine Jane Gutiérrez-Glik, thank you for building home and family together, for giving me the world. The life we have created is beyond my wildest dreams. Everything we have ever done led us to each other. You are the only person who sees me for exactly who I am, every single part of me, and cherishes it all. Thank you for being the best co-mother I could ever ask for, with your love, playfulness, humor, and attunement with our child. I am so proud of your accomplishments, both internal and external. One lifetime together is not enough. And to my child, being your mother is the greatest gift of my life. I believe, with my whole heart, that I have been longing and lonesome for you for most of my life. It is not your job to complete me or make me happy, but simply by existing, you make me whole and happy beyond anything I could have ever imagined. Thank you for being exactly who you are.

And to my clients and consultees, past, present, and future. I don't think you know what you all mean to me. My life has meaning, purpose, and fulfillment because you chose me to share the story of your life with and to include me on your journey of healing. Thank you for choosing me.

NOTES

INTRODUCTION

1. Monnica Williams, Muna Osman, and Chrysalis Hyon, "Understanding the Psychological Impact of Oppression Using the Trauma Symptoms of Discrimination Scale," *Chronic Stress* 7 (January 2023), doi.org/10.1177/24705470221149511.
2. M. T. Williams, M. Osman, J. Gallo, et al., "A Clinical Scale for the Assessment of Racial Trauma," *Practice Innovations* 7, no. 3 (2022): 223–40, doi.org/10.1037/pri0000178.

CHAPTER 1

1. Andrew R. Flores, Ilan H. Meyer, Lynn Langton, and Jody L. Herman, "Gender Identity Disparities in Criminal Victimization: National Crime Victimization Survey, 2017–2018," *American Journal of Public Health* 111, no. 4 (2021): 726–29, doi.org/10.2105/AJPH.2020.306099.
2. Monnica Williams, Muna Osman, and Chrysalis Hyon, "Understanding the Psychological Impact of Oppression Using the Trauma Symptoms of Discrimination Scale," *Chronic Stress* 7 (January 2023), doi.org/10.1177/24705470221149511.
3. Resmaa Menakem, *My Grandmother's Hands: Racialized Trauma and the Pathway to Mending Our Hearts and Bodies* (Central Recovery Press, 2017); Lillian Comas-Díaz and Edil Torres Rivera, eds., *Liberation Psychology: Theory, Method, Practice, and Social Justice* (American Psychological Association, 2020); Mariel Buqué, *Break the Cycle: A Guide to Healing Intergenerational Trauma* (Dutton, 2024); Jennifer Mullan, *Decolonizing Therapy: Oppression, Historical Trauma, and Politicizing Your Practice* (W. W. Norton, 2023).
4. Arielle Schwartz, *The Complex PTSD Workbook: A Mind-Body Approach to Regaining Emotional Control and Becoming Whole* (Althea Press, 2017).
5. Arielle Schwartz, "Complex PTSD and Dissociative Symptoms," *Dr. Arielle Schwartz, PhD* (blog), July 25, 2021, drarielleschwartz.com/complex-ptsd-and-dissociative-symptoms-dr-arielle-schwartz.

6. Jude Mary Cénat, "Complex Racial Trauma: Evidence, Theory, Assessment, and Treatment," *Perspectives on Psychological Science* 18, no. 3 (2023): 675–87; N. Pole, J. P. Gone, and M. Kulkarni, "Posttraumatic Stress Disorder Among Ethnoracial Minorities in the United States," *Clinical Psychology: Science and Practice* 15, no. 1 (2008): 35–61, doi.org/10.1111/j.1468-2850.2008.00109.x; Monnica Williams, Muna Osman, and Chrysalis Hyon, "Understanding the Psychological Impact of Oppression Using the Trauma Symptoms of Discrimination Scale," *Chronic Stress* 7 (January 2023), doi.org/10.1177/24705470221149511.
7. Michael G. Gottschalk and Katharina Domschke, "Genetics of Generalized Anxiety Disorder and Related Traits," *Dialogues in Clinical Neuroscience* 19, no. 2 (2017): 159–68, doi.org/10.31887/dcns.2017.19.2/kdomschke.
8. Maria Shadrina, Elena A. Bondarenko, and Petr A. Slominsky, "Genetics Factors in Major Depression Disease," *Frontiers in Psychiatry* 9 (July 2018): 334, doi.org/10.3389/fpsyt.2018.00334.
9. Nagy A. Youssef, Laura Lockwood, Shaoyong Su, Guang Hao, and Bart P. F. Rutten, "The Effects of Trauma, with or Without PTSD, on the Transgenerational DNA Methylation Alterations in Human Offsprings," *Brain Sciences* 8, no. 5 (2018): 83, doi.org/10.3390/brainsci8050083.
10. Francine Shapiro, *Eye Movement Desensitization and Reprocessing (EMDR) Therapy: Basic Principles, Protocols, and Procedures* (Guilford, 2017).
11. Francine Shapiro, *Getting Past Your Past: Take Control of Your Life with Self-Help Techniques from EMDR Therapy* (Rodale Books, 2013).
12. Daniel Siegel, *The Developing Mind: How Relationships and the Brain Interact to Shape Who We Are* (Guilford, 2020).

CHAPTER 2

1. Lisa Feldman Barrett, *Seven and a Half Lessons About the Brain* (Houghton Mifflin Harcourt, 2020), 30.
2. J. J. Radley, H. M. Sisti, J. Hao, et al., "Chronic Behavioral Stress Induces Apical Dendritic Reorganization in Pyramidal Neurons of the Medial Prefrontal Cortex," *Neuroscience* 125, no. 1 (2004):1–6, doi.org/10.1016/j.neuroscience.2004.01.006.
3. J. D. Bremner, R. Soufer, G. McCarthy, et al., "Gender Differences in Cognitive and Neural Correlates of Remembrance of Emotional Words," *Psychopharmacology Bulletin* 35, no. 3 (2001): 55–87, pubmed.ncbi.nlm.nih.gov/12397879.
4. J. Douglas Bremner, "Traumatic Stress: Effects on the Brain," *Dialogues in Clinical Neuroscience* 8, no. 4 (2006): 445–61, doi.org/10.31887/dcns.2006.8.4/jbremner.
5. L. M. Shin, S. P. Orr, M. A. Carson, et al., "Regional Cerebral Blood Flow in the Amygdala and Medial Prefrontal Cortex During Traumatic Imagery in Male and Female Vietnam Veterans with PTSD," *Archives of General Psychiatry* 61, no. 2 (2004):168–76, doi.org/10.1001/archpsyc.61.2.168.
6. Alastair M. Hull, "Neuroimaging Findings in Post-Traumatic Stress Disorder," *British Journal of Psychiatry* 181, no. 2 (2002): 102–20, doi.org/10.1192/bjp.181.2.102.
7. Lana Epstein, "Putting It All Together: Combining Somatic and Ego-State Therapies with EMDR to Change the Valence of Emotional Memories," lecture, Cape Cod Institute, Orleans, MA, 2018.
8. Phillippa Lally, Cornelia H. M. van Jaarsveld, Henry W. W. Potts, and Jane Wardle, "How Are Habits Formed: Modelling Habit Formation in the Real World," *European Journal of Social Physchology* 40, no. 6 (2010): 998–1009, doi.org/10.1002/ejsp.674.
9. Howard J. Edenberg and Tatiana Foroud, "Genetics and Alcoholism," *Nature Reviews:*

Gastroenterology and Hepatology 10, no. 8 (2013): 487–94, doi.org/10.1038/nrgastro.2013.86; Gunter Schumann, Chunyu Liu, Paul O'Reilly, et al., "KLB Is Associated with Alcohol Drinking, and Its Gene Product B-Klotho Is Necessary for FGF21 Regulation of Alcohol Preference," *Proceedings of the National Academy of Sciences* 113, no. 50 (2016): 14372–77, doi.org/ 10.1073/pnas.1611243113.

10. Michael P. Marshal et al., "Sexual Orientation and Adolescent Substance Use: A Meta-Analysis and Methodological Review," *Addiction* 103, no. 4 (2008): 546–56.

CHAPTER 3

1. Michael D. De Bellis and Abigail Zisk, "The Biological Effects of Childhood Trauma," *Child and Adolescent Psychiatric Clinics of North America* 23, no. 2 (2014): 185–222, doi.org/10.1016/j.chc.2014.01.002; Pierre-Eric Lutz, Arnaud Tanti, Sarah Barnett-Burns, et al., "Association of a History of Child Abuse with Impaired Myelination in the Anterior Cingulate Cortex: Convergent Epigenetic, Transcriptional, and Morphological Evidence," *American Journal of Psychiatry* 174, no. 12 (2017), https://doi.org/10.1176/appi.ajp.2017.16111286.
2. Amanda Doyle, Glennon Doyle, and Abby Wambach, hosts, *We Can Do Hard Things*, podcast, episode 169, "Why We Love the Way We Love: Attachment Styles with Dr. Becky Kennedy," Audacy, January 17, 2023, audacy.com/podcast/we-can-do-hard-things-d7b39/episodes/169-why-we-love-the-way-we-love-attachment-styles-with-dr-becky-kennedy-bd41c.
3. Harvey Karp, *Happiest Baby on the Block* (Bantam Books, 2002).
4. D. W. Winnicott, "The Theory of the Parent-Infant Relationship," *International Journal of Psychoanalysis* 41 (November–December 1960): 585–95, pubmed.ncbi.nlm.nih.gov/13785877.
5. B. F. Skinner, "Baby in a Box; the Mechanical Baby-Tender," *Ladies' Home Journal* 62 (October 1945): 30–31, 135–36, 138.
6. Kerry W. Buckley, *Mechanical Man: John Broadus Watson and the Beginnings of Behaviorism* (Guilford Press, 1989), 162.
7. H. F. Harlow, "The Nature of Love," *American Psychologist* 13, no. 12 (1958): 673–85, doi.org/10.1037/h0047884.
8. B. Ruiz, LCSW, telephone interview with the author, June 2024.
9. Mary D. Salter Ainsworth, Mary C. Blehar, Everett Waters, and Sally N. Wall, *Patterns of Attachment: A Psychological Study of the Strange Situation* (Erlbaum, 1978).
10. Ainsworth et al., *Patterns of Attachment*.
11. Mary Main and Judith Solomon, "Discovery of an Insecure-Disorganized/Disoriented Attachment Pattern," in *Affective Development in Infancy*, ed. T. B. Brazelton and M. W. Yogman (Ablex Publishing, 1986), 95–124.
12. Diane Poole Heller, *The Power of Attachment: How to Create Deep and Lasting Intimate Relationships* (Sounds True, 2019).
13. Robbie Duschinsky, "The Emergence of the Disorganized/Disoriented (D) Attachment Classification, 1979–1982," *History of Psychology* 18, no. 1 (2015): 32–46, doi.org/10.1037/a0038524.
14. L. Hertsgaard, M. Gunnar, M. F. Erickson, and M. Nachmias, "Adrenocortical Responses to the Strange Situation in Infants with Disorganized/Disoriented Attachment Relationships," *Child Development* 66, no. 4 (1995): 1100–6, pubmed.ncbi.nlm.nih.gov/7671652.
15. Judith Solomon and Carol George, *Disorganized Attachment and Caregiving* (Guilford, 2011).
16. E. A. Carlson, "A Prospective Longitudinal Study of Attachment Disorganization/

Disorientation," *Child Development* 69, no. 4 (1998): 1107–28, pubmed.ncbi.nlm.nih.gov/9768489.

17. Harville Hendrix and Helen LaKelly Hunt, *Getting the Love You Want: A Guide for Couples* (St. Martin's Griffin, 2019).

CHAPTER 4

1. Paul Carus, "The Conception of the Soul and the Belief in Resurrection Among the Egyptians," *The Monist* 15, no. 3 (1905): 409–28, jstor.org/stable/27899609.
2. Moshe Miller, "Neshamah: Levels of Soul Consciousness," Chabad-Lubavitch, September 2, 2009, chabad.org/kabbalah/article_cdo/aid/380651/jewish/Neshamah-Levels-of-Soul-Consciousness.htm.
3. Sigmund Freud, *The Ego and the Id*, trans. Hannah Correll (Clydesdale, 2019), 1–66.
4. There's that Western colonial belief again, equating animals with lower forms of consciousness! We must remember how destructive this idea is, and that Indigenous peoples were and continue to be framed as "all Id" or "all animal instinct," in contrast to white, Western culture, which was upheld as logical and moral.
5. C. G. Jung, *The Collected Works*, ed. Herbert Read, Michael Fordham, and Gerhard Adler, trans. R. F. C. Hull, vol. 9, part 1, *The Archetypes and the Collective Unconscious* (Pantheon, 1959).
6. In the 1980s and '90s inner child healing became increasingly popular in the world of pop psychology. Unfortunately, "inner child healing" has been a way for unlicensed practitioners to enter the muddy waters of healing work with clients. We also see this concept used in cults like the Rajneesh movement and other manipulative and unsafe spaces; as inner child work is incredibly deep and vulnerable, it has been used to lower defenses and create experiences of catharsis (big emotional release with no lasting effect).
7. Heinz Kohut, *The Analysis of the Self: A Systematic Approach to the Psychoanalytic Treatment of Narcissistic Personality Disorders* (International Universities Press, 1971).
8. Kathy Steele, Onno van der Hart, and Ellert R. S. Nijenhuis, "Phase-Oriented Treatment of Structural Dissociation in Complex Traumatization: Overcoming Trauma-Related Phobias," *Journal of Trauma and Dissociation* 6, no. 3 (2005): 11–53, doi.org/10.1300/J229v06n03_02.
9. Onno van der Hart, Ellert R. S. Nijenhuis, and Kathy Steele, *The Haunted Self: Structural Dissociation and the Treatment of Chronic Traumatization* (W. W. Norton, 2006).
10. In 1980 a diagnosis based on Janet's theories of fragmented personalities due to trauma became known as multiple personality disorder, and was later renamed dissociative identity disorder (DID). People with DID don't have "multiple personalities" but rather different parts that show up to protect and that don't necessarily know about other parts. People with DID have self-fragmentation to the highest degree because this is what has allowed them to survive their extreme circumstances.
11. Brian R. Van Buren and Mariann R. Weierich, "Peritraumatic Tonic Immobility and Trauma-Related Symptoms in Adult Survivors of Childhood Sexual Abuse: The Role of Posttrauma Cognitions," *Journal of Child Sexual Abuse* 24, no. 8 (2015): 959–74, doi.org/10.1080/10538712.2015.1082003.
12. Ann Polcari, Keren Rabi, Elizabeth Bolger, and Martin H. Teicher, "Parental Verbal Affection and Verbal Aggression in Childhood Differentially Influence Psychiatric Symptoms and Wellbeing in Young Adulthood," *Child Abuse and Neglect* 38, no. 1 (2014): 91–102, doi.org/10.1016/j.chiabu.2013.10.003.
13. Richard C. Schwartz and Martha Sweezy, *Internal Family Systems Therapy*, 2nd ed. (Guilford Press, 2020).
14. Janina Fisher, "Using EMDR with Fragmented Clients: A Protocol for Overcoming

Self-Alienation," slide presentation, EMDRIA Conference (virtual), October 3, 2020.

15. *The Loving Parent Guidebook: The Solution Is to Become Your Own Loving Parent* (Adult Children of Alcoholics/Dysfunctional Families World Service Organization, 2021).

CHAPTER 5

1. Mia Moran, "Activist Angela Davis Addresses Economic, Racial Inequalities in Annual Hesburgh Lecture," *The Observer* (Notre Dame, IN), October 14, 2020, ndsmcobserver.com/2020/10/activist-angela-davis-addresses-economic-racial-inequalities-in-virtual-lecture.
2. Lisa Feldman Barrett, *Seven and a Half Lessons About the Brain* (Houghton Mifflin Harcourt, 2020), 10.
3. Elizabeth Stanley, *Widen the Window: Training Your Brain and Body to Thrive During Stress and Recover from Trauma* (Avery, 2020).
4. Stanley, *Widen the Window.*
5. Deirdre Cooper Owens, *Medical Bondage: Race, Gender, and the Origins of American Gynecology* (University of Georgia Press, 2017).
6. Jennifer Mullan, *Decolonizing Therapy: Oppression, Historical Trauma, and Politicizing Your Practice* (W. W. Norton, 2023), 42.
7. Lillian Comas-Días and Edil Torres Rivera, eds., *Liberation Psychology: Theory, Method, Practice, and Social Justice* (American Psychological Association, 2020).
8. Comas-Días and Rivera, *Liberation Psychology.*
9. Teal Fitzpatrick, "Liberation Work Is Mental Health Care," *No Contact*, February 23, 2021, nocontactmag.com/talking-through/liberation-work-is-mental-health-care.
10. Dean Spade, *Mutual Aid: Building Solidarity During This Crisis (and the Next)* (Verso, 2020).
11. Mia Mingus, "Access Intimacy: The Missing Link," *Leaving Evidence* (blog), May 5, 2011, leavingevidence.wordpress.com/2011/05/05/access-intimacy-the-missing-link.
12. B. Vanessa Coleman, "How Kink Lets Black Folk Get Free: The Liberatory Potential of BDSM," *Salty*, April 20, 2021, saltyworld.net/how-kink-lets-black-folk-get-free-the-liberatory-potential-of-bdsm.
13. Mark S. Friedman, Michael P. Marshal, Thomas E. Guadamuz, et al., "A Meta-Analysis of Disparities in Childhood Sexual Abuse, Parental Physical Abuse, and Peer Victimization Among Sexual Minority and Sexual Nonminority Individuals," *American Journal of Public Health* 101, no. 8 (2011): 1481–94, doi.org/10.2105/AJPH.2009.190009.
14. Lauren Abern, Daniela Diego, Change Krempasky, Jake Cook, and Karla Maguire, "Prevalence of Sexual Assault in a Cohort of Transgender and Gender Diverse Individuals," *Journal of General Internal Medicine* 38, no. 5 (2023): 1331–33, doi.org/10.1007/s11606-022-07900-y.
15. Parice A. Oppliger and Kathryn Mears, "Comedy in the Era of #MeToo: Masking and Unmasking Sexual Misconduct in Stand-Up Comedy," in *The Dark Side of Stand-Up Comedy*, ed. Patrice A. Oppliger and Eric Shouse (Palgrave Macmillan, 2020).
16. Youngmi Mayer (@ymmayer), "me when i'm culturally appropriating my own culture for a bit," Instagram photo, May 23, 2024, https://www.instagram.com/ymmayer/p/C7UzVU_OhP2/.
17. Tamara Santibañez, *Could This Be Magic? Tattooing as Liberation Work* (pub. by author, 2020), tamarasantibanez.com/writing.

CHAPTER 6

1. James Knipe and Jim Knipe, *EMDR Toolbox: Theory and Treatment of Complex PTSD and Dissociation* (Springer, 2014), 5.

2. *Interdependence* acknowledges we need other human beings but honors that we are ultimately responsible for our own happiness, growth, and life. *Codependency* occurs when we either need other people to do for us what we can do for ourselves or do for others what is best done by them.
3. Karlen Lyons-Ruth, Lissa Dutra, Michelle R. Schuder, and Ilaria Bianchi, "From Infant Attachment Disorganization to Adult Dissociation: Relational Adaptations or Traumatic Experiences?" *Psychiatric Clinics of North America* 29, no. 1 (2006): 63–86, doi.org/10.1016/j.psc.2005.10.011.
4. Yu Shi, Lindsay R. Hunter Guevara, Hayley J. Dykhoff, et al. "Racial Disparities in Diagnosis of Attention-Deficit/Hyperactivity Disorder in a US National Birth Cohort," *JAMA Network Open* 4, no. 3 (2021): e210321, doi.org/10.1001/jamanetworkopen.2021.0321.
5. Devon Price, *Unmasking Autism: Discovering the New Faces of Neurodiversity* (Harmony Books, 2022).
6. "Consequences of Bullying Behavior," in *Preventing Bullying Through Science, Policy, and Practice*, ed. Frederick Rivera and Suzanne Le Menestrel (National Academies Press, 2016), https://www.ncbi.nlm.nih.gov/books/NBK390414/.
7. Arielle Schwartz, *The Complex PTSD Workbook: A Mind-Body Approach to Regaining Emotional Control and Becoming Whole* (John Murray Press, 2020), 23.
8. Evelina Käld, Linda Beckman, and Valsamma Eapen, "Exploring Potential Modifiers of the Association Between Neurodevelopmental Disorders and Risk of Bullying Exposure," *JAMA Pediatrics* 176, no. 9 (2022): 940–41, doi.org/10.1001/jamapediatrics.2022.1755.
9. Darren M. Slade, Adrianna Smell, Elizabeth Wilson, and Rebekah Drumsta, "Percentage of US Adults Suffering from Religious Trauma: A Sociological Study," *Socio-Historical Examination of Religion and Ministry* 5, no. 1 (2023): 1–28, doi.org/10.33929/sherm.2023.vol5.no1.01.
10. Alexandra Stein, *Terror, Love and Brainwashing: Attachment in Cults and Totalitarian Systems* (Routledge, 2021).
11. Marlene Winell, "Religious Trauma Syndrome," Journey Free, January 31, 2011, journeyfree.org/rts.
12. At kink and leather community events, sometimes there are people offering to clean leather, like boots, vests, and chaps. This can be an erotic experience or simply a way to meet other people and be educated about how to provide long-term leather care. Bootblacking is both a kink and a hobby.

CHAPTER 7

1. Rachel Yehuda and Amy Lehrner, "Intergenerational Transmission of Trauma Effects: Putative Role of Epigenetic Mechanisms," *World Psychiatry* 17, no. 3 (2018): 243–57, doi.org/10.1002/wps.20568.
2. Rebecca S. Moore, Rachel Kaletsky, and Colleen T. Murphy, "Piwi/PRG-1 Argonaute and TGF-β Mediate Transgenerational Learned Pathogenic Avoidance," *Cell* 177, no. 7 (2019): 1827–41.E12, doi.org/10.1016/j.cell.2019.05.024.
3. Connie J. Mulligan, Edward B. Quinn, Dima Hamadmad, et al., "Epigenetic Signatures of Intergenerational Exposure to Violence in Three Generations of Syrian Refugees," *Scientific Reports* 15 (2025): https://www.nature.com/articles/s41598-025-89818-z.
4. Linda O'Neill, Tina Fraser, Andrew Kitchenham, and Verna McDonald, "Hidden Burdens: A Review of Intergenerational, Historical and Complex Trauma, Implications for Indigenous Families," *Journal of Child and Adolescent Trauma* 11, no. 2 (2016): 173–86, doi.org/10.1007/s40653-016-0117-9.

5. Maria Yellow Horse Brave Heart, "The Historical Trauma Response Among Natives and Its Relationship with Substance Abuse: A Lakota Illustration," *Journal of Psychoactive Drugs* 35, no. 1 (2003): 7–13, doi.org/10.1080/02791072.2003.10399988.
6. T. Evans-Campbell and K. L. Walters, "Indigenist Practice Competencies in Child Welfare Practice: A Decolonizing Framework to Address Family Violence and Substance Abuse Among First Nations People," in *Intersecting Child Welfare, Substance Abuse, and Family Violence: Culturally Competent Approaches*, ed. Rowena Fong, Ruth McRoy, and Carmen Ortiz Hendricks (Council on Social Work Education, 2006), 266–90.
7. O'Neill et al., "Hidden Burdens."
8. Rachel Yehuda, Martin H. Teicher, Jonathan R. Seckl, et al., "Parental Posttraumatic Stress Disorder as a Vulnerability Factor for Low Cortisol Trait in Offspring of Holocaust Survivors," *Archives of General Psychiatry* 64, no. 9 (2007): 1040–48, doi.org/10.1001/archpsyc.64.9.1040.
9. Mariel Buqué, *Break the Cycle: A Guide to Healing Intergenerational Trauma* (Penguin, 2024).
10. Richard C. Schwartz and Martha Sweezy, *Internal Family Systems Therapy*, 2nd ed. (Guilford Press, 2020).
11. Janice A. Sabin, Maddalena Marini, and Brian A. Nosek, "Implicit and Explicit Anti-Fat Bias Among a Large Sample of Medical Doctors by BMI, Race/Ethnicity and Gender," *PLOS One* 7, no. 11 (2012): e48448, doi.org/10.1371/journal.pone.0048448.

CHAPTER 8

1. Emily Coffey, Kate Walz, Debbie Chizewer, Emily A. Benfer, et al., *Poisonous Homes: The Fight for Environmental Justice in Federally Assisted Housing* (Shriver Center on Poverty Law, 2020).
2. Robin Wall Kimmerer, *Braiding Sweetgrass: Indigenous Wisdom, Scientific Knowledge and the Teachings of Plants* (Milkweed Editions, 2013), 166.
3. "Suicide Data and Statistics," US Centers for Disease Control and Prevention, March 26, 2025, https://www.cdc.gov/suicide/facts/data.html; "Drug Abuse Statistics," National Center for Drug Abuse Statistics, https://drugabusestatistics.org/.
4. Laura van Dernoot Lipsky with Connie Burk, *Trauma Stewardship: An Everyday Guide to Caring for Self While Caring for Others* (Berrett-Koehler Publishers, 2009), 41.
5. Sourya Acharya and Samarth Shukla, "Mirror Neurons: Enigma of the Metaphysical Modular Brain," *Journal of Natural Science, Biology, and Medicine* 3, no. 2 (2012): 118–24, pmc.ncbi.nlm.nih.gov/articles/PMC3510904.
6. Marco Iacoboni, "The Potential Role of Mirror Neurons in the Contagion of Violence," in *Contagion of Violence: Workshop Summary* (National Academies Press, 2013), 73–78.
7. Jenny Odell, *How to Do Nothing: Resisting the Attention Economy* (Melville House, 2020).
8. Jenny Odell, *Saving Time: Discovering a Life Beyond the Clock* (Random House, 2024).
9. Tricia Hersey, *Rest Is Resistance: A Manifesto* (Little, Brown, 2022), 7.
10. Odell, *How to Do Nothing.*
11. Qing Li, "Effect of Forest Bathing Trips on Human Immune Function," *Environmental Health and Preventive Medicine* 15 (2010): 9–17, doi.org/10.1007/s12199-008-0068-3.
12. Bum Jin Park, Yuko Tsunetsugu, Tamami Kasetani, Takahide Kagawa, and Yoshifumi Miyazaki, "The Physiological Effects of *Shinrin-Yoku* (Taking in the Forest Atmosphere or Forest Bathing): Evidence from Field Experiments in 24 Forests Across Japan," *Environmental Health and Preventive Medicine* 15 (2010): 18–26, doi.org/10.1007/s12199-009-0086-9.

13. Johanna Hedva, "Sick Woman Theory," *Topical Cream*, March 12, 2022, topicalcream.org/features/sick-woman-theory.
14. Melody Beattie, *Codependent No More* (Simon and Schuster, 2009).

CHAPTER 9

1. Abigail E. Calder and Gregor Hasler, "Towards an Understanding of Psychedelic-Induced Neuroplasticity," *Neuropsychopharmacology* 48 (2023): 104–12, doi.org/10.1038/s41386-022-01389-z.